The Earth Angel's
Healing Guide:

TRUST

YOUR

SENSES

**Worldly Problems,
Cosmic Solutions!**

EXPERIENCED BY: NOVAH'S SON

TABLE OF CONTENTS:

Intro: Dedication to My 1st Love, Mommabear & Sunshine!

Chapter 1: Right Hand of Fellowship: Meditation with Spirit of God & 12 Rays of Consciousness

Chapter 2: Look BOTH Ways

Chapter 3: A Love Chosen

Chapter 4: CHAIN OF COMMAND:

> **Our Mind** = *How we conceptualize thought & hidden triggers into the **Spirit** of Gratitude*
>
> **Our Body** = *Our beliefs, thoughts & actions carried out by our **Vessel***
>
> **Our Soul** = *Embodiment of our BE-ing; Perceptualize as the frequency shift unto our **Mindset***
>
> **Our Spirit** = *Divine experiences of BE-ing; Personified as the **Essence** of our attitude*

Chapter 5: Mind-Full- N.E.S.S

Chapter 6: Defense Mechanisms: Turnin' (L's) Into Lessons

1. Denial | Emotional Imbalance of Judgment & Inferiority
2. Anger | Emotional Imbalance of Clarity & Security
3. Anxiety | Emotional Imbalance of Intuition
4. Jealousy | Emotional Imbalance of Self-Worth
5. Resentment | Emotional Imbalance of Fulfillment, Joy & Divine Abundance
6. Guilt | Emotional Imbalance with Self-Care & Self-Expression
7. Shame | Emotional Imbalance with Self-ID & KNOWING Who TF I AM
8. Self-Doubt | Emotional Imbalance With Self-Love
9. Grief | Emotional Imbalance with Loss & Change
10. Fear | Fear of Disconnection; Losing a Love Never Felt

Chapter 7: Forgiveness

Chapter 8: Intimacy: Into Me Eye See

Chapter 9: Willpower

Chapter 10: Trust Your Senses

DEDICATION

As I journey through this life cycle,
It Was Time For Me To Leave My Tears On These Pages ...

Capturing moments of love as well as gratitude
& I dedicate this book to all of my life experiences.

I give a special "I Life You" to my SUNSHINE.
You are TRULY the love of my life.
I thank you for showing me at 16 years old
how to embrace & GIVE true unconditional love.

To my FIRST LOVE,
"I Love You"
I thank you for giving me a reason
to explore the depth of my heart
through your pure heart, smile & patience.

To MOMMABEAR,
the WOMAN that has always loved
& will forever protect me,
even beyond the veil;
Thank you for encouraging me to see beyond the naked eye.
Thank you for forever holding me up,
no matter how down you were feeling.
I appreciate your strength &
Thank you for showing me mine!

I Love You. I Life You. I Lived For You!

Now, I CHOOSE To Live For Me, Through Me.

THE EARTH ANGEL'S HEALING GUIDE:

RIGHT HAND OF FELLOWSHIP

WORLDLY PROBLEMS, COSMIC SOLUTIONS!

RIGHT HAND OF FELLOWSHIP

Divination Message: July 2021

"For many of you, you are waiting & awaiting…
The right hand of fellowship.
Seeking, hoping, searching & displacing
the truth to be seated amongst the right hand of the Spirit.
To be accepted. Validated. Yet know that we are BLESSED!

Yet we are . . . every time:
We close your eyes to pray
Or bow our head
Enter space of mindfulness to meditate
Or purse your lips to inhale or exhale

As the co creator of our lives,
we are divinely connected to Source energy
in which we have the opportunity DAILY
to fellowship & experience
something welcoming & EXCEPTIONAL!

I encourage you today,
search no more & go within for that which you seek!
As BE-ings of Spirit, connected to Spirit
You Are Source.
You know what's needed, when it's needed.

As nothing outside of you,
is more POWERFUL than you.
& if you truly believe as God,
you know that the Spirit of God beats,
breathes & fulfills PURPOSE WITHIN.

I wanna protect my family, lemme mind the business that pays me.
Not hang out in the streets & do right unto others
as I liked them to do unto me.

I wanna attract ingenuity, lemme release the toxicity I harbor within.
For the folks that have done me wrong, neglected & disrespected me.
Forgive them for messing up with an Earth Angel like myself
& call back my energy in power, universal love,
freedom, joy, favor and purpose.

RIGHT HAND OF FELLOWSHIP

I wanna receive prosperity
lemme call back the wealth of wisdom & abundance.
From my indigenous & Egyptian ancestors,
ritual to cancel our debt from not only my life but my bloodline too.
Call back the energy, blood sweat and tears
of my ancestors and restore faith in the angels
that watch over me and have never faulted with honor

...

DAILY.

-

MEDITATE ON THIS

...

"Image BE-ing in space of consciousness,
that means you're fully aware of your thoughts, actions and presence.
Cleanse & clear your home.
As you do, feel a sense of peace in your mind & then in your body.
So that you align your intent with all YOU LOVE to do thereafter.

Like listen to music, cook or say you love art; so then you paint.

When you're done painting
you are just in awe of your work, design,
your creativity that not only uplifts your face with a smile
but your Spirit with a natural freedom & joy.
Then something gracious overwhelms you.
Coming from a space of mercy, grace, fortitude, faith & GRATITUDE!

So bow, rest your head.
Submit your entire mind, body as well as spirit
in the moment to your creativity and this feeling to embrace.
Getting a true message for its meaning.

In comes the ascended master of the Holy Spirit,
at right in a bright Divine white light energy.
Cupping your head as you are positioned in surrender & steadfast.
Telling YOU, Confirming YOU, Affirming YOU,
"are blessed & your mission is protected".
Then ushering in are the angels. Not just any angels either.
These are the top flight security of the world Craig angels!

RIGHT HAND OF FELLOWSHIP

Encircling you one by one, two by two
with their hands on your back, your sides, your hands, your feet.
& you hear "nobody can speak on the angels like you do."

You experience divine GRACE
as none other than divine GRATITUDE.

Shifting,
Ordering
&
Energizing
your next move is best
& that the journey ahead
you are fully aware & prepared.

Trusting anything you dare question has been answered!
When YOU move, FAITH moves.

Yet,
It is overwhelming.
It is calming.
It is cooling.
It is warmth.
It is peaceful.
It is honoring.
It is exhilarating.
It is pure.
It is yours.
It is complete.

Spread Your Wings Dear Angel."

~ **Novah's Son**

THE EARTH ANGEL'S HEALING GUIDE:

LOOK BOTH WAYS

WORLDLY PROBLEMS. COSMIC SOLUTIONS!

LOOK BOTH WAYS

Look BOTH ways before crossing the street!

I dreamt of a young girl named Gene last night who was crossing the city streets of Bridgeton, NJ. A town within Cumberland County where I'm from in Southern NJ. As Gene crossed the street, she was hit by the NJ Public Transportation City Bus; "553 Bridgeton!".

The bold bus driver was unapologetic, opened the door & yelled to Gene as she laid flat on back alongside the dark, cold pavement; "HEY! Look both ways before you cross the street!".

Because this girl Gene (DNA) was young, college-bound & the energy of my dream felt mothering, nurturing. I jumped out of my sleep & immediately checked on both my daughter & my nephew. They were just fine! SAFE & neither of them had a friend named Gene.

Rather than worry about my kids, I then chose to take a few minutes to divine with Primordial Source energy within & analyze this dream a lil' further. How many times do you do that? Give yourself an opportunity to check in? Check your surroundings? Provide yourself with insight? How often do you just SIT & check-in with your emotions … CONSCIOUSLY?

I went into a unique trance meditation by connecting with the whispers of my breath through the alignment of my body & the energetic embrace of my Spirit. I gave myself permission to connect the subconscious Mind with the conscious Heart & just BE IN SPIRIT.

-

Divination Message: June 2021

"As you check-in with your BE-ing, you give back to yourself with wisdom. Illuminating experiences with gratitude so that you can RESPOND before you react! The material world as well as the spiritual world requires balance.

You get to utilize a significant tool called "discernment" which allows you to decide:
- ☐ What?
- ☐ Who?
- ☐ When? if necessary (ask later - why ONLY if necessary)
- ☐ How? if necessary (ask later - why ONLY if necessary)

LOOK BOTH WAYS

Activating your "Divine Mind" - Your super consciousness, the highest level of your remembrance, BE-ing & mindfulness of your energy. Which prepares you to lead in Spirit, in remembrance, knowing there's "No separation" from Source (creation). It was NEVER meant for society to raise you, nor validate YOU!

As you look both ways, see the past & the future. Recognize the street is PRESENT, utilize your tools & maintain your presence.

Into the grounding of your mission, appreciate your perspective, remaining non-judgmental as you illuminate your light in situations of darkness & chaos. Through discernment, maintain self-mastery with confidence as well as compassionate healing. Above all else, utilize self-discipline. Practice inner-strength daily with the heart of mindfulness & unconditional love to continuously maintain your own vibration & raise that of all that you interact with.

The mission is living within the expansion of higher frequency as Primordial Source Energy. Choose to relax your mind, body, spirit & essence into this knowing & enjoy your life."

~ **Novah's Son**

-

With clarity, the path is clear yet there's always risk. A chance something that appears to come from out of nowhere that grabs our attention. To cultivate universal alignment within establishes the remembrance of knowing how to MOVE WITH PURPOSE so that we don't get hit.

With intention, we look both ways to honor the past & respect we're from yet distinguish to implement our future that's no longer where we are nor where we go to elevate. The road ahead leads with an abundance of inner-peace, personal power, mental focus, compassion, self-worth, kindness to others & the healing power transmutation within as well as around us.

It's essential to set boundaries for balance by nurturing a cleansed environment & preserving the alignment of our energy!

LOOK BOTH WAYS

ALWAYS remain aware of your energetic fields:
(KEEP TRACK IN YOUR JOURNAL!)

- [ ] Embrace Oneness
- [ ] Slow Down, Time Is Energy
- [ ] Lead With Spirit
- [ ] Experience Lessons With FAITH As Blessings
- [ ] Grow & Evolve Without Fear
- [ ] Find Your Joy & Fulfillment in Mystery
- [ ] Radiate Unconditional Love
- [ ] Shine Your Light
- [ ] Experience GRATITUDE
- [ ] Divine Alignment; Always STAY Connected!
- [ ] TRUST YOURSELF!

SET NEW GOALS EVERY YEAR: BE INTENTIONAL
(or as often as you need)

Reframe the Mindset to YOU

- [ ] Connect with your energy authentically & truthfully
- [ ] Practice discernment with your values as well as emotions

Self-Expression

- [ ] Use creativity to connect within
- [ ] Embrace your emotions
- [ ] Apply wisdoms of emotions from a healthy space & build healthy relationships

Experiencing GRATITUDE

- [ ] Releasing negative vibrations
- [ ] Innerstand your grace / power
- [ ] Attract ABUNDANCE: Knowledge, Wisdom, Prosperity & Love

Celebrate yourself DAILY!

REMEMBER THIS ***
If you do not do it in the privacy of your own home, why do it in the public of society?

LIGHT MEDITATION:
(Surround SELF with light; Go Within & Embrace YOU)

-

Before you start going to bed every night & as you rest in power;
I want you to start envisioning a bright white protective light circled around your whole body.

Reflect on everything or anybody that you no longer choose to have in your life
Or those that you may feel as blockages in life …
See these outside this encircled light, no longer having access to you!
No longer being attached to you!
No longer being in your energetic field,
Nor being allowed in your sacred, protective space.

Upon waking, as you rise in power.
See the things your heart desires within your protective light.
Whether it's something physical or not.
Peace, money, a new car, quality time, etc.
Embrace with protection, healing & love trusting that it's already received.

-

**Use this as a protective shield to rest your mind at night
as well as a daily meditation to set your intentions each day.**

**Start doing this every day!!!
Be consistent.
Know there will be ups & downs.
Yet keep going & trust your journey!**

LOOK BOTH WAYS

SELF-LOVE MASSAGE:
(I AM Love, I AM Light)

"She has a light & knows HOW TO USE IT!"

Your spiritual journey is non-negotiable.
Replace the "IFs" with WHY.
Diminish the "ANDs" with DISCERNMENT.
Then Eliminate ALL the "BUTs"!

As you create rituals for your journey, remember this…
You're required to EMBODY your light energy within your vessel.

Embodiment is the actions of your soul,
aligning within your mission of PURPOSE.

Create a List:
WAYS TO GIVE BACK
💕

consider ways that you can
SHOW UP
as your true self amongst humanity sharing your
GIFTS,
TALENTS,
SKILLS
OR
VOICE.

Seal this list in an envelope.
Hold this to your heart & embrace it.
Envision living life, within fulfillment & prosperity.
State the following affirmation aloud,
"I AM Love, I AM Light"
For the next 3 days,
Place the envelope under your pillow.
REST IN POWER!

THE EARTH ANGEL'S HEALING GUIDE:

A
LOVE
CHOSEN

WORLDLY PROBLEMS, COSMIC SOLUTIONS!

A LOVE CHOSEN

One day, I asked the woman I was falling in love with "What do you do when your biggest fear is also your greatest gift?" & her response was "Embrace It".

Little did she know mine was giving & receiving compassionate love...

I feared love without reciprocity, although I know I am soulfully created to love beyond condition.

As fear, it was terrifying for me to express that this woman I had manifested; I saw within my future as my wife. This person I instantly connected with, I desired to build a legacy with. The woman I'm attracted to flaws & all, I felt safe with in her arms. To see her, know her & love her for who she truly is, as myself.

As fear, it was terrifying for me to express that I see her mirrored as my soul. Yet, I had already decided as it was divinely guided that we'd meet & I would CHOOSE to love. I chose to analyze the toxicity often associated with forming as well as maintaining relationships. Starting with SELF.

When it comes to giving & receiving, I had to acknowledge the self-sabotaging behaviors I create over the years of childhood trauma, influenced pain from past lovers & misguided mistrust within friendships as well as other relationships alike. These manipulated bridges, mountains & walls preconceived as restrictions & limitations preventing the flow of unconditional love.

As a gift, I was chosen to embrace love within my Spirit. Applying what it felt like to fall in love without emotional barriers constructed as defense mechanisms to prevent inevitable pain.

Experiencing the energy of divinity & self-love with confidence in remembrance. Deciding not to allow outside negative influence to diminish the strength as well as power of the subconscious mind. Nor reflect conscious living of my behaviors, actions & responses to life. I stand in the remembrance that

"I will not allow the circumstances to diminish the abundance of my reality"!

~ **Novah's Son**

I was no longer choosing to allow emotional pain to keep me in bonadage from my growth & evolution as FULL POTENTIAL OF BE-ING.

THE EARTH ANGEL'S HEALING GUIDE:

CHAIN OF COMMAND

WORLDLY PROBLEMS. COSMIC SOLUTIONS!

CHAIN OF COMMAND

I reference the "INNER-standing" of oneself seeing as we innerstand our Chain of Command through the ritual of self-love. We acknowledge not only the time yet the patience as well as care for self that is required to NURTURE what it is that our mind & heart truly desires as it aligns & connects.

As we become self-aware, we initiate a divine connection between the rationality of our calm thoughts & the determination of our rejuvenated bodily responses. As well as the endurance within our mental focus & the serenity that surrounds the functioning of the body. Creating a harmonic rhythm inside & out as we lead with spirit. Putting who we are called to be on the forefront of EVERYTHING we say as well as all that do.

We often self-exploit a great battle among this intellect directed as our Chain of Command. Becoming intimate with dimensions of consciousness within our BE-ing in the equilibrium of our SPIRIT, SOUL & VESSEL as we manifest our EXPERIENCES creates unexpressed fears. Without confronting these fears we curate unnecessary burdens of stagnated beliefs, a lack mindset & ultimately an intangible war. A fraternizing war within the structure of our mental, emotional & physical functioning that hovers a misconceptualized shadow unto our Quantum field. Leaving one to inquire "Whose real demon(s) we are fighting but our own?".

**In divine alignment we connect the mind, body, soul & spirit
as one source of energy unified unto Faithful Sense.**

-

Our Mind = *How we conceptualize thought & hidden triggers into the **Spirit** of Gratitude*
Our Body = *Our beliefs, thoughts & actions carried out by our **Vessel***
Our Soul = *Embodiment of our BE-ing; Perceptualize as the frequency of our **Mindset***
Our Spirit = *Divine experiences of BE-ing; Personified as the **Essence** of our attitude*

-

The Quantum Field, epitomizes the illuminated energy space within cell membranes of the body as well as the magnetic shield protectant amongst our Aura that which we embrace our full potential. The field in which we CHOOSE (*pay attention to how many times I use a word that confirms how we are the SOURCE ENERGY to authorize a decision in our life*) openly accept as well as receive healing, create freely as self-expression, then manifest the desires of the heart through intangible & tangible joy as well as fulfillment.

CHAIN OF COMMAND: SPIRIT

(Source Connection Expressed as Divine Gratitude)

Lead With Spirit:
An Awakening of Gratitude

As we nurture our BE-ing, we must configure & evaluate our daily routine on a DAILY basis. Before getting out of bed, we must begin by asking ourselves each morning...

How do I choose to "<u>Spiritually</u>" RISE IN POWER?

- [ ] What Do I Choose To Express Gratitude For?
- [ ] How Do I Choose To Experience Gratitude Today?
- [ ] How Will I Honor & Value Self?
- [ ] Who Are My Spirit Guides?
  - [ ] And Have I Thanked Them For Their Guidance/Protection?
- [ ] Have I Connected With My Highest POWER Within?

TOOLS to Raise Your Vibration:
1) Each morning affirm rising. Call back your Energy, Power & Money unto YOU!
2) Peering towards the east with the Sun, unto your soul (your spirit, your highest level of consciousness, your divine light within) give honor & thanks, state *"I thank you Spirit for a new day & new opportunities to rise as the Spirit of my FULL POTENTIAL."*
3) Define your "GRACE" for self. Set intentions for your daily goals.
   - **TIP** - Prioritize functioning by highlighting your tasks of the day. Choose the TOP 3 goals to complete before the end of the day. With mindfulness & time management, align your BE-ing to start your day with a plan of action designated for completion. Allow flow with grace, confidence & execution. If there's room for more, do more.
   - **TIP** - Do not allow the hiccups whether small or big to interrupt your vibration.
4) RISE IN POWER, speak uplifting affirmations/mantras to SELF in a mirror.
   - **TIP** - If needed, throughout the day . . . REPEAT! REPEAT! REPEAT!

*** Live in Faith | Trust the unseen; your intuition, oversoul & Spirit Guides

CHAIN OF COMMAND: SPIRIT

EXERCISE: Own Your Shift!

GOAL:

☐ Identify unexpressed or suppressed areas of fulfillment.

☐ Give these energetic spaces a name.

☐ Acknowledge a timeline, presence & depth for transition.

☐ Give focus, thanks & appreciation to the spaces that create joy.

ASK YOURSELF - Does my current DAILY routine support me spiritually, mentally, emotionally as well as physically?

- Spiritual Daily Routine

- Mental Daily Routine

- Emotional Daily Routine

- Physical Daily Routine

19

CHAIN OF COMMAND: SPIRIT

CHAIN OF COMMAND: SOUL

(Self-Love Paradigm Shift)

Lead With Spirit:
Nourish The Soul

As chaotic as it can be, we'll briefly explore the depth of our Subconscious Mind. The Garden in which we plant seeds that heavily influence & often determines our reaction or response amongst the unknown. The Conscious Mind functions as The Gardener in which we authorize the application of our actions as well as response amidst surrender to the flow or the knowing. Paradigms are a collection of thoughts, habitual behaviors and perceptions outside of our BE-ing that dictate our INNER feelings, trusted action, experience and outcome. Shines empowerment into the creation & transparency of our subconscious or conscious shifts.

The grand news is that we get to CONTROL the narrative of our BE-ing & decipher which parts of ourselves to embrace as well as that which to relinquish.

-

Divination Message: June 2021

"SOUL TALK - Lean into the discipline of wholeness & oneness. Do not remove SELF from this space. When feeling ungrounded or unbalanced, know to look towards the "Sun" in the East! Seen or unseen. Known or unknown, call upon guides of this direction. Embrace the healing of Archangel Raphael as Earth energy. The presence of growth. Richness. A youthful heart that's simultaneously wise, forgiving as well as joyful. Restore purpose & mastery unto the heart's center every time you're in need!"

~ **Novah's Son**

-

Establishing a divine connection with AA Raphael supports the healing process with grace & abundance. Therefore, do not be scarce! Rather be intrigued by the realization of hope.

When guidance is what we seek, ASK. Reap the wisdom to heal, then recognize the wealth that surrounds our circumstances. Utilize this knowledge to transfer empowering energy as a unique blessing.

CHAIN OF COMMAND: SOUL

TOOLS to Raise Your Vibration:
1. Set a reminder for the day that empowers the BEST version of SELF & prompts conscious living:
   - Affirm, *"I release all that no longer serves me, as I journey into this day with a peace of mind & grace within my experiences."*

2. ACTIVATE SOUL TALK. Conversations with SELF that lean into self-discipline for the order of wholeness guiding the mind & oneness stimulating the body.
   - This form of restoration builds a connection with our healed beliefs, therefore we do not remove SELF from this space of mastery.
     - **TIP** - When feeling ungrounded or unstable look towards the Sun, embracing your light within & energetically pull yourself into PURPOSE. Envision yourself outside in nature with tree roots expanding from the soles of your feet into the Earth. Affirm *"I AM HOME."* - Recite 3(x)s.
   - Trust the journey. Explore what feels good in divine alignment for you, despite the seen or unseen.

3. Share stories of your growth in a space of peace & gratitude.
   - Consider empowering expressions of creativity that incorporate your enlightenment.
     - Writing a Blog or Book
     - Post videos for a YouTube Channel or Social Media LIVE
     - Schedule speaking engagements: *(start locally, spread nationally)*

*** Live In Faith | Whether in thought or as events, uproot then diminish negativity & toxicity with a self-care regime

CHAIN OF COMMAND: SOUL

EXERCISE: Decipher the difference of your beliefs & values contemplating what you were taught vs what you profoundly learn about yourself in consciousness.

GOAL: Decide what you'll choose to keep as wisdom of your BE-ing.

ASK YOURSELF - What stimulates my "Emotional" balance? What enhances the well-BE-ing of my consciousness?

☐

☐

☐

☐

☐

☐

☐

☐

CHAIN OF COMMAND: SOUL

CHAIN OF COMMAND: SOUL

CHAIN OF COMMAND: VESSEL

(Self-Care: Accountable Actions & Responsive Behaviors)

Lead With Spirit:
Determine How You'll Choose To Show up!

It's the APPLICATION for me...

Often we use prayer as a way to talk, plead, talk some more. Sending endless requests or commands to what some refer to as Spirit or some call God without the consciousness to actually BE still & listen for a response...

YET,

!? When do we open ourselves up mindfully to hear the answers?
!? How long do we await receipt of healing, joy or fulfillment?
!? How often do we neglect to align with our vibration of the expected results?
!? When do we just breathe, hush up... & LISTEN; for divine guidance!?

Mindfulness is a POWERHOUSE!

An energetic connection of soul fulfilled guidance within our purpose that collaborates our physical being & our spiritual essence as one.

With a daily mindfulness practice you will not only uniquely understand, but you will begin to accept as well as interpret the divine wisdom your body, your mind, your soul and your spirit embodies within as a sacred tool to receive the healing in addition to blessings of divine favor.

GRACE & EASE.

*** Live In Faith | Water the challenges of life with the sequence of your FULL potential

CHAIN OF COMMAND: VESSEL

RISE IN POWER
with a cleansing meditation

SHOWER MEDITATION

***

Create Divine Connection
Pair with Your Awakening. Deep inhales. Deep exhales.
Unto your Divine Light within as Source of highest consciousness.
Unto the planet Mercury as "The Messenger" & communicator of the cosmos.
Unto the element of water as it is a conduit to cleanse, flow & release a message.
Evoke a protective shield of light encircled around the body & aura.
(you can choose a white light or color that supports your intent)

***

1st WASH - Fully cleanse your body with mild soap & warm water.
As you commence to an initial cleanse, meditate on your goals or intention.
Ask Yourself: **HOW DO I CHOOSE TO RISE IN POWER?**
(I prefer to use a herbal soap with essential healing properties as peppermint or rose)

2nd WASH - As you cleanse yourself with intention;
Contemplate an outcome of completion as heart fulfillment with a mindset of abundance.
Create statements affirming protection, healing, evolution, love, prosperity, etc.
Recite as words of power for each corresponding chakra in universal alignment & wealth.
(chakras are our energetic wheels within the vessel)

RINSE - Under the warmth of the water, center your BE-ing in faith.
Seizing the completion of your results as it's already done.
Unveil all attributes of conscientious nature that you feel through the breath.
Pair with fulfillment. Deep inhales. Deep exhales.
*(receive with trust & confidence that the essential powers of the water have
cleansed any toxic energy with light & fulfilled your manifestation as pure love)*

Recite Grounding Chant. (pg. 34)

CHAIN OF COMMAND: VESSEL

EXERCISE: Hidden Triggers Prevent Growth & Evolution

GOAL: Acknowledge any self-sabotaging barriers created from past trauma or pain that you currently use as a way to relate with others.

ASK YOURSELF - Do I harbor residual, unhealed emotions that repeatedly penetrate the outcome of my manifestations as well as BE-ing?

- [ ]
- [ ]
- [ ]
- [ ]
- [ ]
- [ ]
- [ ]
- [ ]

CHAIN OF COMMAND: VESSEL

CHAIN OF COMMAND: EXPERIENCES

(Wisdom Gained from Personal Interactions)

Lead With Spirit:
What am I learning through the depth of SELF?

It is not until we have lived that we truly can say we have learned ourselves. By scrutinizing our mannerisms, demeanors, morals, words & ideologies we determine whether or not we've created patterns that may avoid our internal conflicts.

Examining my past attitudes & conduct, I recognized that I utilized binge eating as a mechanism for concealing overwhelming anxiety & emotional turmoil. By stuffing my mouth with salty, sweets & comfort food, I compromised self-expression by suppressing the mind-boggling thoughts & events consuming my mental capacity. Creating a level of self-sabotage within my body that slowed down my energetic fields as well as physical functioning. I began blowing off responsibilities to mask temporary emotions that created clutter not only as mental brain fog but also a visible mess within my home of piled dishes, clothes, papers & other unorganized items.

Inwardly, this level of self-inflicted toxicity collectively overexerted my mind, body & spirit branding an unnecessary rise of restlessness. Dominating feelings of insufficiency, consequently I began over studying, overworking & overextending my BE-ing in domains where it wasn't demanded. Intentionally leaving room to ruin relationships with loved ones. All because I repeatedly feared & attempted to avoid having uncomfortable conversations.

Confronting my greatest fears & mindfully overcoming the depth of my anxiety with not only words of power yet audacity, diminished deficiencies within my mindset as a black woman that was raised to feel seen rather than heard.

Get a feel for the things you are MOST fearful of?

TOOLS to Raise Your Vibration:
1. Sit in prayer then meditation & acknowledge the presence of any challenges (-) you may be experiencing with INNER-standing. Create a surge of beneficial (+) energy by intentionally shifting your perception. Affirming unto your results or outcomes it's ALREADY DONE!

*** Live In Faith | Command Your Essence: Uproot with transparency, Resoil in understanding & Be Rooted as awareness!

CHAIN OF COMMAND: EXPERIENCES

MEDITATION

Close your eyes & connect to the breath of your Spirit.

Begin to feel the rhythm of your heart.

Deepen your inhale (*counting 4, 3, 2, 1*)
& lengthen your exhale (*counting 4, 3, 2, 1*). REPEAT - 3x(s).

Envision a bright white protective light surrounding your younger self in your PJs, standing at the end of the driveway to your childhood home.

Embrace the first memory that comes to your mind. Do not pull back. Do not force it.

Allow the memory to connect you with remembrance.
Who you were as a kid, how you felt & what you truly needed
within the memory of that very moment.

Ask yourself, *"What do I want? What do I need?"*

Redefine your emotional support as well as spiritual connection & give your younger SELF a unique message that invokes CLARITY & FULFILLMENT. Place your focus on what you now desire with grace & ease, rather than what was or could've been as trauma & pain.

Nourish your newfound affinity & seal your message with a strong, calming hug.
Feel an energetic release that captivates your BE-ing in all dimensions
(past & present) with inner peace.

Illuminate the embodiment of peace by encircling both your younger self
as well as present self with the healing light.

Hold this visualization until the embrace naturally dissolves.

Recite Grounding Chant. (pg. 34)

CHAIN OF COMMAND: EXPERIENCES

EXERCISE: Connect & review ways to independently heal & balance your "BE-ing".

GOAL: Determine your current perspective & if you endured a shift from an unhealthy mindset.

ASK YOURSELF - WHOLE-listically what are my 7 goals of mindfulness?

- [ ] Spiritual Goals - Unlearning what you've been taught & Relearning you're divine connection to Spirit

- [ ] Educational Goals - Knowing the difference between knowledge & wisdom as well as the application of discernment

- [ ] Emotional Goals - Promoting support & balance within healthy independence

- [ ] Relationships - Creating healthy boundaries while utilizing discernment & releasing unhealthy attachments & bondage

- [ ] Finances - Releasing fears of lack & shifting into a mindset of worth, abundance & prosperity

- [ ] Wellness - Surrounding ancestral. Generational healing. Holistic healing.

- [ ] Business / Career - Connecting purpose & prosperity to obtain fulfillment & euphoria. Combining material world & spiritual world

CHAIN OF COMMAND: EXPERIENCES

CHAIN OF COMMAND

Divination Message: December 2020
(You're going to want to bookmark this page!)

You never know when you need tools for balance & grounding,
therefore as you encounter those unique & enchanting resources;
EMBRACE THEM WHOLEHEARTEDLY!

This chant came to me repeatedly as I was awakening from an astral dream state.
As soon as I woke up, I had completely forgotten what I was reciting verbatim.

I was upset at first.

I knew that it would come back me, so later that afternoon on my lunch break
I sat in meditation, opened my BE-ing to receive & asked Spirit to support my remembrance.

I closed my eyes & within minutes, I began this meditative chanting once again . . .

THIS TIME, I IMMEDIATELY WENT TO WRITE IT DOWN AS NOTE IN MY PHONE.

GROUNDING CHANT

Sacred in My Purpose.
Sacred in Truth.
Sacred Amongst All Others.
Divinely Guided & Protected.
Grounded in the Beauty of All Things on Earth.

THE EARTH ANGEL'S HEALING GUIDE:

MIND
FULL
N.E.S.S

WORLDLY PROBLEMS. COSMIC SOLUTIONS!

MINDFULNESS

MINDFULNESS: *(Mind - FULL - of Necessary Energetic Synchronicities from Spirit)*

Creating a ritual of stillness within the subconscious & conscious mind through a combination Spirit-led experiences of serenity, unity & mastery as your highest level of conscious BE-ing. Connecting the mind to the body, body to spirit & spirit to essence of faith.

LEVELS OF MINDFULNESS
1. Meditation - Mind
2. Contemplation - Body
3. Centering - Spirit of the SELF

MEDITATION - *"Sit Down"; Hands over ROOT CHAKRA (base of spine)*

- [ ] Permission we give ourselves as we relearn it's ok to sit down & revitalize
- [ ] Just let go & allow SELF to just BE, in the present moment
- [ ] Find solitude & silence as the most authentic & natural state of BE-ing
- [ ] Learn to BREATHE. Release fears, worry, anxiety, doubt, scarcity through the power of the breath.
- [ ] Allow daily sacred time of rest, reflection as well as liberation
- [ ] Grounding. REPETITION IS REQUIRED! Repetition is a key component.

CONTEMPLATION - *"Shut Up"; Hands over THROAT & HEART*

- [ ] Connect with the body's center, the heart space. Gain emotional support from within.
- [ ] Do not overthink. Just embrace what is presently felt.
- [ ] The state of reflection in which we not only gain a deeper insight but CHOOSE not to immediately react.
- [ ] Allow the knowledge to invite clarification & transparency.
- [ ] Trust that our voice & heart combined, are our doorway to wisdom.
- [ ] Connection with gratitude & truly experience gratefulness.
- [ ] Where we inhale positive vibrations & blessings, then exhale tension, stress & bullshit!

CENTERING - *"Open Up"; Hands over CROWN & ZEAL (Top of head & nape of neck)*

- [ ] Trance state of experiencing euphoria. Inner joy.
- [ ] Accepting the moment to BE PRESENT
- [ ] Creating calm & balance. Inner peace & strength within.
- [ ] Self-discipline with grace. Giving self opportunity to have fun & be joyful. Experience HARMONY!

MINDFULNESS

- [ ] Flow of empathy & divine gratitude through the heart center.
- [ ] "Zeal Chakra" is also known as "The Mouth of God" or "The Ascension Chakra". It is located at the nape of the neck where the Vagus Nerve & the Medulla Oblongata meet. This sacred space connects to an INNERstanding of clairvoyance, perception & love. Hosts as a gateway to express CHRIST CONSCIOUSNESS.

EXPERIENCE, ENJOY & EMBRACE JOY!

TOOLS to Raise Your Vibration:

- [ ] RATE 1-10 | How Important "I AM" to SELF?
- [ ] Journal Prompts:
    1. My HIGHER SELF wants me to know _____ ?
    2. My IDEAL daily routine is _____ ?

Divination Message: June 2018

Original motto, received vibrationally as a dream unto me.
I woke up from a meditative sleep reciting these words over & over again without fail.
Upon launching my reiki candle line in 2020, I created both a business along with
a meditation card using this unique message of grace as words of power for every order.

> "I am my highest self.
> So I will be my higher self.
> Connected mind, body, soul.
> Energetically, Spiritually & Vibrationally.
> Serving to learn, grow, teach &
> Share with compassion."

~ **Novah's Son**

TOOLS to Raise Your Vibration:

- [ ] Journal about the vibration you receive from reciting this meditative affirmation.

THE EARTH ANGEL'S HEALING GUIDE:

DEFENSE MECHANISMS: (L'S) INTO LESSONS

WORLDLY PROBLEMS. COSMIC SOLUTIONS!

DEFENSE MECHANISMS

Let's chat defense mechanisms!

These are those annoying & let's be honest manipulating fear-based thoughts, provoked into feelings then coached as our beliefs, raising sabotage unto our existence. It is from the impediments of our environment over time that we encumber seeds of fear & pain. We are conditioned to exist in fear by experiencing change as loss. Yet born in spirit as Spirit, we are birthed as pure consciousness sanctioned unto certainty, affluence & delight.

This is where we ASK OURSELVES:
What keeps ME from ME ???

-

**ALL THAT IS SUPPRESSED
or swept under the rug.**

In death, we were taught to grow attachment unto the physical body of our loved ones.
In poverty, we were taught to materialize our success, worth & abundance.
In relationships, we were taught that as they dissolve we experience loneliness & bitterness.
In business, we were taught that without accreditation we do not acquire knowledge.

Digging all up & through those old beliefs, I've learned from pain, childhood trauma, unspoken words, etc. lead to a "mask". The masks were often displayed as negative reactions portrayed out of unexpressed fear. Defense mechanisms develop as inarticulate subconscious despair, assuming I can diminish or seduce my emotional pain with temporary sensations that hinder growth & furthermore evolution. Especially as I endorsed frivolous character habits that may evolve into impulsive toxic personality traits.

Quick tempered anger, flared jealousy, fleeting anxiety, triggered emotions, etc.

Via forethought, seeds of fear & pain plant roots unto courage that grows a tree of stillness as well as forgiveness. Strengthening the branches in which we may extend release & support balance. In addition to the flourishing of bountiful leaves we radiate in abundance as compassion, intellect, restoration & harmony.

REMEMBER THIS ***
There is no evolution in pain. You gain insight & will, along with self-discipline from the teachings of our collective interactions.

DEFENSE MECHANISMS

EXERCISE: Through the next few pages with each listed below, create a list of your known "Defense Mechanisms" that you may have subconsciously created in fear to protect or suppress emotional pain that keeps you from growth & evolution.

- [ ] Denial
- [ ] Anger
- [ ] Anxiety
- [ ] Jealousy
- [ ] Resentment
- [ ] Guilt
- [ ] Shame
- [ ] Self-Doubt
- [ ] Grief

Meditate on the notion that they ALL STEM FROM FEAR!

GOAL: Uproot your Defense Mechanisms with accountability. As you begin to reveal the obvious, notice the obscurities that flow through to the surface. Give yourself room to acknowledge, accept & receive your sentiments without blame or judgment.

ASK YOURSELF - CONSIDER WHICH OF THESE PLAYS THE BIGGEST ROLE AS FEAR IN YOUR LIFE?

_____
_____
_____
_____
_____
_____
_____

DEFENSE MECHANISMS

THE EARTH ANGEL'S HEALING GUIDE:

DEFENSE MECHANISMS: DENIAL

WORLDLY PROBLEMS. COSMIC SOLUTIONS!

DEFENSE MECHANISMS: DENIAL

Denial operates as fear with a hint of procrastination that generates a network of blockage, if it remains unhealed. With denial we face emotional scarring from judgment & inferiority, yet let's examine who stipulates these ideals onto our spirit. Innerstanding that words are power; we ALLOW the mind to receive what uplifts with LIFE & REBIRTH or that which casts spells of DEATH & DESPAIR over our BE-ing (actions & energy).

Around 10 or 11 years old, experiencing sexual abuse began the disconnection for me from not only the trust often exchanged as intimacy but also the physical connection with others. By avoiding the reprimand of result or lingering in disbelief, I can account a multitude of events throughout my life in which I allowed the manipulation, deceit, & misguided energy of my desires to manifest as:

- Unsolicited experiences
- Unconsented sexual encounters
- Overextension of baneful attachments
- Emotional turbulence
- Escapism or Self-Sabotage
- Adversity to forward movement
- Pride & Retaliation
- Lack of self-awareness
- Limited thought patterns
- Restricted possibility

(... Clearly, at some point I was just a HOT ASS MESS ...)
- But aren't we all? -

As I enabled stagnation, this dramatic unexpressed notion of unease constantly regurgitated mental, emotional & physical walls brick by brick. As bad as I wanted, needed & was required to shift cause & effect onto my circumstances, in hindsight I realized the energy I was creating & expressed ONLY imploded as denial the more I suppressed what I believed were infiltrating emotions.

Denial appeared repetitively in my life mentally as layers of avoidance, victimization, entitlement & interrupted sleep patterns, met with what I thought were nightmares. Yet those "nightmares" typically indicated underlying fears of my karmic past projecting into the future. The mental combat poured out as night sweats, sudden awakenings with incomplete dreams, random outbursts or crying in dreams, constant heart palpitations, even a sense that this "darth vader" presence is hovering me. I felt unsafe & inferior.

Later I learned this shadow blazing the scene, lurking before me was my veil & gift of truth. Awaiting my grasp. For me to take the reins & advocate. Repurposing its presence amongst the light of adversity. It is only through our darkness & dark times that we illuminate opportunities to BE STILL. Reflecting what has been of goodwill in our lives as well as what has not. In these moments, I learned to release self-judgment & how to create GOOD through Divine WILL!
This is how you remember that "I AM" ... The Source & Power within to prevail.

DEFENSE MECHANISMS: DENIAL

GOAL: Uproot denial with ACCOUNTABILITY. As you begin to reveal the obvious, notice the obscurities that flow through to the surface. Give yourself room to acknowledge, accept & receive your sentiments without blame or judgment.

ASK YOURSELF - WHEN DO I JUDGE MYSELF THE MOST, DUE TO FEAR OF INFERIORITY?

- [ ]
- [ ]
- [ ]
- [ ]
- [ ]
- [ ]
- [ ]
- [ ]

DEFENSE MECHANISMS: DENIAL

EXERCISE: Determine how you may punish the SELF consciously or unconsciously?

Create a (Denial) Statement
GOAL: Analyzing actions & negative thinking patterns & transmuting through healing statements of power

ASK YOURSELF - Do you have trouble accepting the parts of YOU that are unspoken, malnourished or unhealed?!

☐ FINISH the following statement - (Denial Statement)
- I have trouble accepting _____ about myself.

_____
_____
_____
_____
_____
_____
_____
_____
_____
_____
_____
_____
_____
_____
_____
_____
_____

DEFENSE MECHANISMS: DENIAL

EXERCISE: Determine how you may punish the SELF consciously or unconsciously?

Create a (Releasing Denial) Statement
GOAL: Releasing unhealthy attachments, grudges & experiencing true forgiveness of SELF

ASK YOURSELF - What do I honor about SELF?

- [ ] FINISH the following statement - (Releasing Denial Statement)
    - I love, accept & value _____ about myself.
    - Utilize this statement to create a 30-60 sec video with 10 things you love & honor about SELF?

THE EARTH ANGEL'S HEALING GUIDE:

DEFENSE MECHANISMS: ANGER

WORLDLY PROBLEMS. COSMIC SOLUTIONS!

DEFENSE MECHANISMS: ANGER

WHERE THE HELL WAS MTV WHEN I WAS 16 & PREGNANT ???

"One of my most distinctive memories I can recall is being about 4yrs old at the K-Mart on Delsea Dr. with my Mommabear & my two favorite Titi(s). We had just moved into our FIRST HOME where I get my own room & mother is of course adding her pazazz."

We FINALLY get to the home decor section with all the pretty colored towels & wash rags (I love bright colors). I'm getting away with touching EVERYTHING to see which brand has the softest thread count. Now, usually this is not a thing (I damn sure couldn't do this two aisles ago). Mother makes me hold onto the cart, so what's different at this moment? Why do I get to touch & play in the store? Right now?

*Next thing you know, I hear **"Chelle take meh fuckin' purse! Derla grab meh damn pickney!"**.*

*It wasn't long after that I saw Mommabear walking up on her, snatching her up, flipping her over & banging her head into the towel rack, then dragging the woman down the middle of the store by her hair. After punching on this pale-faced lady & yelling at this woman to leave her fuckin' husband alone or else she'll beat her ass every time. My Mother smooths out her blouse, grabs her purse, my little hand & tells my Titi(s) **"Let's go!"**. She waltzes out of the people's store leaving our cart of home goods & my colorful picks towels & wash rags for our new house.*

It was like everyone moved out of the way for us to leave. NO managers, NO cops, NO nothing.

Nobody wanted these types of problems ... EXCEPT this dumb ass lady!

WHO?!

Oh! The pale-faced lady that lived down the street from Mount Pisgah Methodist Church, Home of my Godfather Reverend Oliver. Daddy sometimes took me to her house while Mother was at work. I mean I thought she was nice because she did my hair & it made me feel pretty. Afterwards she gave me her remote control & her & Daddy went down to her basement, so I got to watch ALL my favorite cartoons & shows. My older sister & brother never let me watch what I wanna watch so Daddy makes sure I have ME TIME! I just guessed Mother didn't like that but as I got older I saw it was MUCH DEEPER THAN THAT... "

My brother always tried to keep me out of sight when they argued or fought, however some things I could not escape. Such rage & anger displayed through the walls of Sawyer avenue made me believe growing up that THIS is what "love" was supposed to be like....... RIGHT?

DEFENSE MECHANISMS: ANGER

When I was 12, Mommabear finally divorced Daddy. Not just because of his cheating with the pale-faced women, but come to find out he also liked sleeping with underaged girls too. Needless to say, *finally* having my own room in our own home did not last long. We were back living apartment to apartment within 5-6 years later. At this juncture, I embedded in my subconscious that I wouldn't allow my kids to feel this level of infuriating disappointment & implicit resentment from ***any relationship***. In hindsight, losing my safe space, my own bedroom and walk-in closet, our fresh garden, our 3 pure-bred Labradors and my security is what stuck with me. The fascinating adventures of my imagination day by day slowly diminished & early on I faded into this despair of unconscious self-sabotage.

Throughout Elementary, Middle & the very beginning of High School I was an overachiever. I intentionally buried my mind & body with things that just "kept me busy". I focused on straight A's, often being teased for being the teacher's pet. I joined the choir to sing my blues away, praying no one heard the pain through my Soprano tone. I participated in D'Ippolito's School band, that's when the baritone horn was my best friend... My ONLY friend. What I thought was being content in my skin with ponytails, overalls & printed tees as confidence later revealed to me as suppressed anger. I did not attempt to stand out, I enjoyed my crab shell..... Maybe a little too much!

Creating this stigma of infatuating betrayal within, caused me to detach from all relationships. Not only with women & femininity, yet men as well as self-discipline & structure, the divine union. If I couldn't even trust my parents to keep me safe & grounded, who the fuck could I trust, so... TRUSTED NO ONE & that fear .... made me BITTER and ANGRY!

Then BAMMM! The summer before 8th grade I met "Chocolate". Chocolate was my first love, my first REAL boyfriend, my first relationship... My FIRST everything!

He made me feel like I was the only person that matters in his world & at times my own world. I felt my self-confidence erupt. I noticed how tone changed whenever he was around. My voice was calm, clothes were tight & short and my love language spoke volumes that were often deafening. There were times I craved just having a conversation, because I knew "Hey Beautiful, how was your day?" would end up in eight hour uninterrupted face to face conversations.

Two-years later is when it all came around full circle.

I finally lost my virginity and let "Chocolate" taste my chocolate. Within eighteen months, I was sixteen and pregnant by the same person who impregnated my cousin. Granted he swears he didn't know we were related when he met her, however we look and act just alike. I mean damn, I sang my heart out to Brittney & The Spice Girls with this heffer! The more I thought about it, the more disrespected I felt allowing ANGER, RAGE & utter betrayal from women & men exploded in what now was then my fat face and swollen feet ALL OVER AGAIN!

DEFENSE MECHANISMS: ANGER

My daughter IS my greatest blessing from that relationship, yet I have done without the 10 years on and off again bullshit, the constant nagging & bickering, the physical altercations and my FIRST miscarriage. By 19, having to start a NEW job with a busted lip & after the set of twins outside of our relationship were born, I FINALLY called it quits. I no longer settled to question whether "THIS is what LOVE was supposed to be like……. RIGHT?" - *I chose NOT to settle for insecure love.*

DEFENSE MECHANISMS: ANGER

GOAL: Uproot ANGER with Self-Respect & Security. As you unravel the layers of the emotional body, you will have found hidden narratives in which you've agreed to settle vs awaken your joy. Consider what brings you the MOST joy & schedule time Weekly, Monthly, Quarterly & Annually to JUST DO IT!

ASK YOURSELF - WHERE DO I LACK SELF-RESPECT, DUE TO FEAR OF TRANSPARENCY?

- [ ]
- [ ]
- [ ]
- [ ]
- [ ]
- [ ]
- [ ]
- [ ]

DEFENSE MECHANISMS: ANGER

EXERCISE: Reflect on the powerful influences that have shaped the way you view your INNER World as well as the OUTSIDE World around you.

GOAL: Redefine how you desire to present SELF to the community with soul power?

ASK YOURSELF - What were the most IMPACTFUL relationships, growing up? How do you see the effects in your life currently?

☐ Negative?

☐ *Inner Vision?*

☐ Positive?

☐ *Inner Vision?*

☐ Neutralize Your Experiences with HARMONY?

DEFENSE MECHANISMS: ANGER

THE EARTH ANGEL'S HEALING GUIDE:

DEFENSE MECHANISMS: ANXIETY

WORLDLY PROBLEMS, COSMIC SOLUTIONS!

April 18th, 2009, after wrapping up my paper route around 4am that morning, something told me to actually READ the damn newspaper...

I had spent the last four hours delivering about twelve-hundred of these suckeers house to house & Wawa to Wawa and didn't even realize my ex-boyfriend had made headlines in The Daily Journal for murder.

As I'm crawling back in bed with the newspaper & my coffee, my mouth drops open to see the baby daddy of my third unborn child in the Crime Section under the headline *"Camden man charged with shooting death of Millville resident"*.

I immediately jumped out of bed & threw "Foreign Motors" the nakedness lying next to me, their clothes. I specifically remember waking Foreign Motors out of their sleep abruptly saying "You gotta go, I can't do this & YOU at the same time... WE'RE DONE!". I tossed the newspaper section & in less than two minutes later up and out the door was Foreign Motors... NO QUESTIONS ASKED.

With just a glimpse down at the photo & a few keywords from the headlines, we BOTH knew my heart was unsettled yet content on doing a "bid" with someone I could've sworn I'd love for life.

Since Dark Chocolate, I had been emotionally unavailable in relationships and made that VERY CLEAR with whoever I was shacking up with. Yet here goes Vanilla Cream, taking my breath away... Literally.

People definitely warned me to NOT get involved & at the time I knew I shouldn't have either. Afterall who in their right-mind had the balls to stare me down while their girlfriend is less than a foot away? Yet the intriguing nature of Vanilla Cream's actions made me want to have my coffee stirred even more. For the first time in a long time, it excited me inside & out to be desired in such a way. Courteous enough to not have me in no drama... That particular day that is, yet BOLD enough to confirm "I'm going to make you my wife!"

This relationship became a game of monopoly real fast.

I was a giddy twenty year old, that allowed a seventeen year-old fresh out of the juvenile detention center to infiltrate my life. I had the most to lose, a four year-old daughter. I'm supposed to be her role model & yet there I was RISKING IT ALL to feel something... The potential of ANYTHING!

I didn't listen to my friends, family nor my gut when she said "Just f*ck em & leave, Have Fun!". I did not trust myself enough to NOT fall in lust and every time we were alone, I fell deeper. It wasn't the person I fell in love with. As a giver and an empath, naturally I fell in love with "The Potential"... The potential to improve this youngin's norm outside of Juvi by experiencing my love. When you know that you are created with love, you tend to wanna spread love everywhere you go. Overtime that gets old, especially when you do not TRUST your own intuition, you often displace what you know to be compassion with infatuation.

The morning I read the headlines, was the day I self-inflicted mental anguish due to mistrust. I wanted to believe that Vanilla Cream would have FINALLY been faithful to loving me and ONLY ME, if I had shown them that I'd ride this jail sentence out. I spent the next two years running back and forth to 2 window visits a day, spending thousands of dollars on five minute phone calls five times a day, and weekends hustle contraband in my vagina. It wasn't until I noticed the calls were far & few in between, the visits went from one a day to randomly canceled with ten second phone calls and I love you was no longer our second language that I became aware I was being deceived.

Such agonizing betrayal, *"How do you cheat on someone from f*ucking jail?"*

It disturbed me how I sat outside Cumberland County Jail for three months watching other b*tches filter in and out during what used to be our time to connect BEFORE I finally said "This isn't my life!"

I believe I had to FEEL the pain, FEEL the mental clutter, FEEL the heartache to INNER-stand THIS isn't life. I was merely existing in a plot, a scheme of sorts, and I wanted out. I wanted out so much that I attempted suicide not once but twice! I felt so unloved, unlikeable, pressured & defeated by failure because I wouldn't rise to a space of "knowing" & living so I chose to EXIST. I was available for everything & everybody else and remained unavailable to not only myself, but my Womanhood. The Nurturer within me. The Creator of Life. The Facilitator of Awareness & Truth. The Mother of Clarity and The Goddess of Joy. I had almost forsaken life because I wouldn't see through the INNER treachery & OUTER disloyalty that I ultimately created... One morning after reading the damn newspaper.

It was the second attempt driving home New Year's night 2011 that encouraged me to EXPERIENCE exactly what I deserved more of... LIFE & PURPOSE.

Being blacked out drunk behind the wheel, longing to die & STILL making it home safely by the grace of Spirit, instantly gifted me insight & prophecy. I HAVE PURPOSE and until my mission is complete, my purposeful ass was here to overcome these f*cking human emotions through Life, Death & Rebirth.

I let go of what no longer served me... I released the jail sentence with Vanilla Cream's ass. Ultimately relinquishing the burden and hold I had placed on the chambers of my rainbow pyramid because when the heart screams LOVE is not corruption! It's time for a change.

DEFENSE MECHANISMS: ANXIETY

Love is Kind and Patient.
Love is Pure and Filling.
Love is Truth and Abundant.
Love is Joy and Expressive.
Love is Forgiving and Trusting.

My next stop on this love train was renewed in St. Paul, Minnesota ... So I thought!

DEFENSE MECHANISMS: ANXIETY

GOAL: Uproot anxiety with TRUST and SELF-AWARENESS. The Power of Meditation gifts you the ability to GO WITHIN. We often seek prayer, talking to a God outside of our BE-ing vs Ritualing with Meditation so that we may hear & listen to the Spirit of God within.

ASK YOURSELF - WHEN WAS THE LAST TIME YOU NEGLECTED YOUR INTUITION, DUE TO FEAR OF THE UNKNOWN?

☐

☐

☐

☐

☐

☐

☐

☐

DEFENSE MECHANISMS: ANXIETY

Divination Message: March 2022

"Divine As I AM.
Divine in my Might.
Continue to bless me,
With the Divinity of The All Sight."

~ **Novah's Son**

If the Spirit will do nothing else, the Spirit will gift you with divine compassion.
It is the human experience that exudes benevolence reshaping our wisdom within.

Through experience you amplify consciousness, recognition and discernment.
When we are forthcoming about the experience, we gain value through our personal memoirs.
Asking the SELF, "what does this teach me",
rather than focusing on what's egotistically offered to compensate.

With rare appreciation,
we have the Power within to collectively as well as individually
SEE BEYOND LIMITATIONS!

DEFENSE MECHANISMS: ANXIETY

EXERCISE: Place your hands over your heart & invite higher knowing to guide you through what is required to be RELEASED so that you can embody the Divine Courage to experience life's hidden and unknown treasures with grace and ease. Uproot anxiety through SELF-AWARENESS and MEDITATION.

GOAL:

☐ Uproot stagnant energy from your life cycles.

ASK YOURSELF - What "I AM" willing to let go. What must I allow to EXPERIENCE & EXPAND?

- Mind

DEFENSE MECHANISMS: ANXIETY

- Body

DEFENSE MECHANISMS: ANXIETY

- Spirit

THE EARTH ANGEL'S HEALING GUIDE:

DEFENSE MECHANISMS: JEALOUSY

WORLDLY PROBLEMS. COSMIC SOLUTIONS!

DEFENSE MECHANISMS: JEALOUSY

I had a "friend" call me & tell me that she was jealous of me... Jealous of my spiritual development, growth and wisdom because that's what they wanted to cultivate in their life. This was NOT my first encounter of jealousy with self, family, coworkers nor friends, yet I decided in THIS moment it would be my last.

Rather than run into a shell, cut them off, dismiss their feelings or instantly become defensive, I CHOSE to do what was required & that's to inquire. I CHOSE to practice involution for evolution & asked what made her feelings of inadequacy a notion of jealousy between us. Once we openly communicated without a mask, I realized TRUTH & truth is we've all been there before. Once you've been through something & notice the patterns, it's ESSENTIAL to uproot the cause.

Self-worth & free will play a combative attraction to divine fulfillment. Often we people watch & consider what our own life would be like "IF we could " or "I WISH I can"...

After our conversation, privately as well as in a group setting she then proceeded to ask me for my guidance in strengthening intuition and although I felt this co-dependent energy, naturally I AM always willing to guide even when I learn! I choose to be of service where I AM invited, yet when my services were extended NO RESPONSE was avail. I knew then, this was yet another co-dependent friendship in this karmic loop and this time I'm required to flow with dissolution and healing.

As an empath accommodating this human experience, what appeared to be a confession or moment of truth was absolutely NO SURPRISE to me... You learn to connect with all energy & it is through self-healing & self-reflection you build keen insight & clairsentient as to who and/or what is for YOU and what isn't.

The energy, behaviors and inconsistency rooted in lack and envy is NOT for Earth Angels. As we are claircognizant BE-ings and we connect to an ALL-KNOWING sense of certainty that allows one to SHIFT energy as necessary.

AFFIRM, DECLARE & DECREE:
"Release the karmic cycle of inadequacy from all timelines, spaces, relationships & dimensions!"

Jealousy is often the fear of not knowing or APPLYING who we are called to experience. So you may victimize self, patronize or idolize others, sometimes pick apart what you assume to be their flaws, goals, accomplishments or what you think they lack when there's really a void missing within you.

In reality, the subconscious mind recognizes they're living how you desire to BE, yet you become so focused on them that you may quickly forget YOU CAN CREATE the same "FOR YOU, THROUGH YOU!" You may miss opportunities to fulfill your purpose if you are too focused outside of you.

Because after all, who's stopping you from BE-ing YOU?!
If you are so busy watching others move, you may want to ask yourself "Where AM I going?!"

DEFENSE MECHANISMS: JEALOUSY

The moment you DECIDE to own your worth, you then own your BE-ing. You transform lack to wealth & abundance uprising your consciousness by BE-ing the leader of your life as well as guide for others. Pay attention to where your energy flows. Notice where the vibration around you <u>authentically</u> contributes to your Highest Self as well as notice what genuinely liberates life through self-mastery.

Universal Principles develop, connect & maintain your I AM PRESENCE with Christ Consciousness with an essence of "ALL THAT GOD IS I AM, FOR I AM ALL THAT GOD IS".

This illumination of BE-ing allows ONE to live a fulfilled life in love, peace, productivity, protection, abundance & grace guided from within. Honoring as well as trusting Divine Will of the Spirit. The Principle of Vibration culminates in an energy of receiving. Vibration affirms energy is in constant motion, never ceases yet filters & redistributes. Much like kinetic energy, vibration applies to matter but also one's personal frequency as well. This principle states that our vibrational frequency (choice of thinking & believing) may inform as well as influence our lived experiences.

CONSIDER THIS:
You may have something good in life but can you keep it?
Are you steadily sustaining a feeling of growth, mindfulness, potential and optimism?

HOW TO APPLY: *The Principle of Vibration*
Maintain an elevated frequency through uplifted energy. Practice being more present and being more mindful in ALL that you do. Try a sound bath, chakra clearing, Reiki, meditation, etc., whatever you choose; be sure you ALLOW everything to FEEL more enjoyable.

PAUSE! & ASK YOURSELF "What energy do I want to emit while I am doing THIS?". Fully immerse yourself by releasing resistance and resentment from any situation or opportunities. When we choose to SHIFT our focus as well as view we tend to look beyond the physical eye & see through the energies of manifestation. You may see into the keys of creation such as release, forgiveness, self-reflection, gratitude and optimism. Trust they are there, often within a VOID, awaiting YOU to fill your sacred spaces.

What will you ALLOW relinquishing so that the burdens you've created & carried for so long are FINALLY shed free from your mind, body and spirit. Giving room to do as you LOVE. Giving way to honor more of what you CHOOSE to value, respect and bless into your DAILY LIFE.

Throughout the human experience, that's what we're called to do ……………… Let shit GO!

WITHOUT malice.
WITHOUT hidden narrative.
WITHOUT friction.
WITHOUT circumstances…
NO CONSEQUENCES!

DEFENSE MECHANISMS: JEALOUSY

Creating an unconditional compassion for SELF to release the barriers as well as unhealthy boundaries we attempt to shield our BE-ing with.
This provides us with the willingness to be compassionate for all others.

*** REMEMBER THIS: What you create in the mind, forms in the body and leads as the Spirit!

DEFENSE MECHANISMS: JEALOUSY

Divination Message: February 2021
(Master Keys for Unbreakable Liberation)

Often we may unconsciously attach ourselves to subjects outside of ourselves as we attempt to connect, identify & relate to our INNER relationships and/or love. You may find yourself overcompensating, overspending, overdoing, overworked, over the edge and constantly overwhelmed!

You may very well just need a mental workshop...

> *"I relax and cast aside all mental burdens, allowing G.O.D to express through me. Perfect love through my Spiritual Gifts, peace of INNER-standing & Oneness and apply wisdom as truth through Discernment."*

- **Novah's Son**

DEFENSE MECHANISMS: JEALOUSY

Consider whether you're "BE-ing Relatable in your Relationships". How do you show up? Whether it's with your partner, your friends, your family, your spouse, your parents, your children, your coworkers, hell roommates.

The most important relationship to consider is:
How do you show up "<u>for</u>" as well as relate "<u>through</u>" SELF?!

Mull This Over:

DETACHMENT - Do you detach from your ego with negative resistance mentally & emotionally when faced with opposition.

- If not, choose to recognize & understand the energy. As it is often unconscious; Is it compulsive? What happened earlier that day? Are you displacing upset or confusion elsewhere?

    ☐ GROUND YOURSELF!
    ☐ IDENTIFY WITH SELF!
    ☐ CONNECT WITH TRUTH!

Try to root your emotions by journaling or find enrichment with self-talk exercises in a mirror.

SURRENDER - Ok so catch this tea...
NO ONE HEARS YOU, IF AT FIRST YOU DON'T SHUT UP & HEAR YOURSELF.

- If you desire willpower, seek CLARITY! Within...
- If you require inner peace, be TRANSPARENT!

    ☐ The combination of one's unique experiences & the creativity of their expression delivers a spiritual strength like no other. Leaving room for opportunities of nonjudgmental, non-bias, open and honest communication.

DEFENSE MECHANISMS: JEALOUSY

COORDINATION - When aligning with others, remember it is STILL your sacred space, so don't sugar coat shit! INNER-stand that goal is to create HARMONY & UNITY!

Even if this is not Uno or Solitaire know that solitude is essential to self-reflect ...
INNER-stand the relationship you create within is not a game as it will create your reality around you.

Trust that when you're really ready to form a connection, bond, relationship or community you will attract like-minded individual(s) that desire to HEAL, strive to ELEVATE and have the similar GOALS and achievements as you. Your relationships will feel inspiring & no one person is a winner.

Each person will CHOSE to participate in their evolution as well as yours.
Create genuine gratitude from this energetic connection DAILY!

Don't try to MANIPULATE your circle!
Do I have to explain?!
I hope not ...

If you have to lie, cheat, steal & hustle your way into a relationship of any kind...
HOW LONG DO YOU THINK IT'S GON LAST?
Or how much of that do you have to keep up to maintain it?!
YES! Even w/ SELF!

CONSISTENCY - Take ACTION! Be present in the "now" DAILY.

- How you CHOOSE to show up for self reflects in ALL your relationships!

    - ☐ Hold space for expansion & new opportunities.
    - ☐ Be open to accepting & receiving Universal support.
    - ☐ Have the courage to grow.
    - ☐ Master your peace to let go.

DEFENSE MECHANISMS: JEALOUSY

GOAL: Uproot jealousy with FREE WILL & ADVENTURE. Allow Spirit to work as guidance & the Universe to flow with favor as well as abundance.

ASK YOURSELF - WHAT AM I REQUIRED TO ALLOW, TO RELEASE JEALOUSY AS FEAR?

- [ ]
- [ ]
- [ ]
- [ ]
- [ ]
- [ ]
- [ ]
- [ ]

DEFENSE MECHANISMS: JEALOUSY

EXERCISE: AFFIRM: I AM the grace & ease of divine freedom, fulfillment & joy.

GOAL:

☐ Have the courage to release those things that you no longer need, and that are preventing you from growing.

ASK YOURSELF - WHAT AM I REQUIRED TO SURRENDER?!

1. Stand in front of a mirror naked.
2. Place your hands over your heart; Left then Right.
3. Deep breaths - Inhale Light, Exhale Love!
4. As you stare into your Third Eye (space between the brows), recite 7x the following affirmation "I AM the grace & ease of divine freedom, fulfillment & joy."
5. Breathe into your brilliance. Deep breaths - Inhale Light, Exhale Love!
6. Shake your hands out once done!

JOURNAL: NOTE HOW YOU FEEL THEREAFTER?! Then create a list of 5 things that FILL YOU UP with inner peace & joy.

_____

_____

_____

_____

_____

_____

_____

_____

_____

_____

_____

_____

_____

_____

DEFENSE MECHANISMS: JEALOUSY

THE EARTH ANGEL'S HEALING GUIDE:

DEFENSE MECHANISMS: RESENTMENT

WORLDLY PROBLEMS. COSMIC SOLUTIONS!

DEFENSE MECHANISMS: RESENTMENT

We've all heard the phrase "Deja Vu", RIGHT?

Have you felt like you've been HERE BEFORE, wherever HERE is?
Have you ever met someone new then felt like you've known them for a LIFETIME?
Have you ever had a feeling that this is FAMILIAR, whatever THIS is?

YES! Yet, what is Deja Vu?

Metaphysically deja vu is reoccurring karma rooted in unfulfilled disappointment. Through spiritual enlightenment we decide to allow the wisdom produced through experiences to determine our conscious decisions as well as motivate SELF-Acceptance.

Whenever I experienced stress, struggle or tension in life as resentment, I tend to revert to a poverty mindset. What did that look like... Let's dive in!

- [ ] Unhealthy eating habits
- [ ] Spending before receiving OR Overspending
- [ ] Isolation
- [ ] Overworking OR Under shadowing my gifts
- [ ] Neglecting responsibilities OR Avoidance
- [ ] Paranoia OR Assumptions
- [ ] Judgment of self AND others

All of these actions related to a DEEP insecurity with finances as well as my relationship with money.

Money is currency. Money is an energy that's stimulated or rejected by our emotions. When one holds onto resentment, there's this undignified envy within circulating fury which leads to malignant energy as well as non beneficial behaviors. It's essential to realize that YOU HAVE THE POWER OF CHOICE. Holding onto any anger or bitterness may generate inner turmoil & Dis-Ease. Ponder in stillness to determine where the root cause is buried so that you become FREE within to confidently release it!

Reflect on WHY something & someone may have wronged you, especially if that someone is YOU!

Be sure to allow yourself patience and sit with the hurt or discontent so you can then CHOOSE TO ACCEPT, THEN FORGIVE. Try contemplating on several redeeming qualities that attracted & stimulated or may have repelled & rejected such recurring events as well as emotions. This is where inner work culminates high vibrations & circulates the energy of good fortune.

Growing up with Caribbean parents & after divorcing my Dad, my Mommabear worked 2-3 shifts a day managing to "survive" with three teens on her own. Me being the youngest of the three, I resented the

DEFENSE MECHANISMS: RESENTMENT

majority of my childhood especially throughout my teenage years as I spent a lot of my life "feeling" alone. This conditioning of loneliness led me to believe that without adequate guidance or compassion directly from my Mom, I'd ALWAYS long & yearn for love, security and support.

Yes! I had my Sistabear & Brothabear who are my ride or die(s).
Yes! I had my cousins, who were my best friends.
Yes! I had my Titi(s), who looked out for me & at one point to me in their homes.

My family always seemed to be around me or with me, so I often questioned…
WHAT'S MISSING?
WHY DO I STILL FEEL THIS EMPTY VOID?

> *There were times in which I felt like a burden versus a purpose…*

I bottled up my feelings, my trauma and ALL inner frustrations with lack, self-worth, much like my Mommabear did when she was being cheated on & physically abused. Much like my siblings who experienced their own childhood trauma, depressed & suppressed their emotions. Feeling defeated, I grew to be an antagonist of the truth.

> ***The truth is, all that I had been conditioned to DID NOT BELONG TO ME!***

Although we try to run or hide from the authenticity of our true nature, it has a way of rearing its head, exactly when we're required to receive. It is not until we CHOOSE to attain courage, face the depth of life's imperfections that we may create abundance as well as celebrate reality within "The Void".

> *You are TODAY where*
> *Your thoughts have brought you.*
> *You will be TOMORROW where*
> *Your thoughts take you.*
> *- James Allen -*

Self-acceptance is one key that ignites FAITH & PROSPERITY. As one proclaims divine conviction, know that faith is a state of mind grounded by the universal principle of inspired action. Such a fulfilling as well as powerful ritual builds voluntary positive habits. What calls to us in the body as emotional intelligence fills the application & overflow of forgiveness through self-discipline, perseverance, resilience, willpower, and faithfulness. Through this flow of energetic coding we may create faithful prosperity unto our Divine Soul Mission.

This I affirm, declare & decree is "FAITHFUL SENSE"!

DEFENSE MECHANISMS: RESENTMENT

GOAL: Uproot resentment with ACCEPTANCE.

ASK YOURSELF - WHERE DO I STAGNATE LACK, RESTRICTIONS & LONELINESS IN MY CURRENT EXPERIENCES?

☐

☐

☐

☐

☐

☐

☐

☐

DEFENSE MECHANISMS: RESENTMENT

Our "personal pyramid" embraces the heart chakra as the master of unconditional love & compassion. It is through acceptance that we are capable of awakening mastery within others. Throughout the human experience we must align in oneness and choose peace to illuminate the heart center. This level of consciousness shines with a pure white vibration through interactions with others captivating the 33 chambers of unconditional love.

EVERY evening before you go to sleep, utilize the following meditation to cleanse your energy.

- Focus on releasing; Set intent.
- Invite in goodness and grace; inner peace

(in your personal pyramid)
I invite you invoke the Violet Flame and recite to yourself or out loud:

"I decree to release cause, core, record and memory of ALL discordant energy I have ever created, past, present and future, in this or any other reality. **SO BE IT! - SO IT IS! - IT IS DONE!"**

1. See the Violet Flame blaze up from beneath your feet, or around your body if you are lying down.
2. Envision the Violet Flame bathing you in its transforming Light throughout your bodily form to its innermost core.
3. Then send the Violet Flame down into the crystalline caves within the Earth, which contain the eternal Violet Flames.
4. Envision it moving throughout the labyrinths in your area and sweeping throughout the totality of the Earth.

DEFENSE MECHANISMS: RESENTMENT

EXERCISE: Write a letter to your younger self. What advice & encouragement would you give him/her?

GOAL:

☐ Apply in your current experiences ALL that you required to receive THE MOST throughout your childhood.

ASK YOURSELF - What advice would I give my younger self? GO DEEP… CREATE GRATITUDE & RELEASE!

_____

_____

_____

_____

_____

_____

_____

_____

_____

_____

_____

_____

_____

_____

_____

_____

_____

_____

_____

_____

_____

_____

DEFENSE MECHANISMS: RESENTMENT

THE EARTH ANGEL'S HEALING GUIDE:

DEFENSE MECHANISMS: GUILT

WORLDLY PROBLEMS, COSMIC SOLUTIONS!

DEFENSE MECHANISMS: GUILT

I am absolutely no saint & I do not project myself to be as I have done some pretty shitty things in my life due to lack of self-love. Including yet not limited to being 16 and pregnant by someone who also impregnated my paternal cousin. As well as through moral turmoil, sleeping with my maternal cousin's boyfriend every chance I could get out of spite.

It didn't matter if I met him first & felt betrayed by my own blood. Nor did it matter that my own blood slept with my "side nigga" & then told him about my boyfriend before I slept with hers………….

In hindsight, what should've mattered the most was that I was self-sabotaging with temporary satisfaction through suppressing my childhood trauma & abandoned emotions for far too long.

Subconsciously we create an image of ourselves to the world in which we seek to be validated, seen and understood. MOST of the time that shit gets all entangled & ass backwards because we often misrepresent on the outside when, what & how we really FEEL on the inside. Forgetting that our perception unto the world is truly a reflection of just how we represent the SELF.

Metaphysically "Guilt" conceptualizes the misrepresentation of our good, our truth, our light within.

In this, "Guilt" becomes the fear of communicating with an outer voice as well as emotional barriers we self-inflict neglecting to sustain rituals of self-expression and self-care. In the event you leave a gap that lacks self-discipline, discernment & perception… With unhealthy boundaries, our frequency of SELF-LOVE remains an empty void filling with unsolicited opinions & antagonizing guilt.

When I was about nine or ten years old, my parents separated & all my Mom's kids had to separate and live with a different family member. I stayed with one of my favorite Titi(s). The one that is always a ball of fun & plans the gatherings, parties or family vacays!

She lived at a dead end, which was a circle… Whenever I felt boxed in, displaced or out of place by some event happening through my youthful & naked eyes (which was often), I went outside to the circle. I kicked around rocks, made up words that became a song to express how I felt inside. I would close my eyes & just sing whatever came flowing out my mouth from my heart…

I'd imagine myself anywhere but HERE!
Anywhere but straddling with despair, dysfunction & dis-ease weighing on my shoulders.

Visualizing myself mentally & emotionally & spiritually happier. Hoping that my mom, my brother & sister, and our lives were physically wealthier & financially healthier. These visualizations helped me cope with physical, sexual & emotional abuse, because at the time they were just imaginary spaces for me.

DEFENSE MECHANISMS: GUILT

As I grew in the wisdom of my experiences, I learned sacred circles represent wholeness & I have the power within to recall & APPLY meditative visions into my current timeline of reality. Knowing and essentially feeling that I can be all that my mind creates & my heart leans into with inspired action.

I was BE-ing led to focus more on Divine Fulfillment & actively pursuing "What bring me JOY!"

It wasn't until my mid-twenties & two suicide attempts later that I decided, rather than remain stuck by karmic loops & society, I MUST amplify my goals, visions & dreams with the purpose to LIVE FREE.

Allowing The Self to envision the greater aspects of a life fulfilled empowers actionable behaviors to attain your goals as well as amplify supply. When we harbor our inner voice, peace then becomes disturbed with an unsettling fear & control. That lack of self-control leaks into our digestive system & every time we encounter an experience or someone that attempts to restrict one from inner knowing & inner truth our gut sends a signal of discomfort, pain or imbalance to steer us into alignment.

Whether that may come as emotional distractions, boredom, nausea, cramping, stomach ulcers, addictions (substance or emotional), lower back & pain & other digestive related issues or unfulfilled sensuality as well as sexuality or sexual pleasure.

We truly must LET "SHIT" GO, no pun intended to be FREE inside.

As we set boundaries for self as well as with others, we learn to move through indiscretions with pure joy, love, grace & ease. It was through self-sabotaging experiences that I get to prioritize the following healthy boundaries FOR ME, THROUGH ME:
1. I will give myself time to receive the flow of my full potential daily.
2. I will not allow outside circumstances to overwhelm me & choose to honor my own true feelings.
3. I will prioritize my work with adequate time, mindfulness & emotional availability.
4. I will detach from all things to rejuvenate in wholeness with Source when guided & required.
5. I will allow gratitude to evolve the wisdom of ALL my experiences as blessings.
6. I give my power space to elevate, create & prosper as my TRUE NATURE of Divine Success.
7. I choose to frequent space with nature to ground as my soul's mission integrates on this Earth.

Always BE OPEN to possibility & affirm "I allow clear pathways to Know that my work is "GOOD" in the vibration & Spirit of Self-Love!

DEFENSE MECHANISMS: GUILT

GOAL: Uproot guilt with HEALTHY BOUNDARIES.

ASK YOURSELF - What are principles of life that you refuse to negotiate with? Consider values you are not required to control as well as that you can not live without…

- [ ]
- [ ]
- [ ]
- [ ]
- [ ]
- [ ]
- [ ]
- [ ]

DEFENSE MECHANISMS: GUILT

EXERCISE: Write a list of "regrets". One by One DECIDE what you will take away to keep & what you will give back to Source for healing & transformation.

GOAL:

☐ Create self-expressions of gratitude for every experience that once was perceived as negative or toxic.

ASK YOURSELF - What has this experience taught me?

DEFENSE MECHANISMS: GUILT

THE EARTH ANGEL'S HEALING GUIDE:

DEFENSE MECHANISMS: SHAME

WORLDLY PROBLEMS. COSMIC SOLUTIONS!

DEFENSE MECHANISMS: SHAME

Much like guilt, shame requires one to lead their life with healthy boundaries yet it's within the courage to RELEASE that we elevate & CREATE shameless BE-ing.

Here's a list of things & life occurrences I once was ashamed & fearful to portray as my TRUTH:

- [ ] **My Body**
    - *After being teased about my 8-shaped figure as a kid & multiple misconceptions.*
- [ ] **My Natural Hair**
    - *After being called "nappy-headed" as a kid.*
- [ ] **Being Homeless**
    - *After trying to entertain & impress others.*
- [ ] **My Crooked Smile**
    - *After being punched in my mouth by some guy I barely knew.*
- [ ] **My Businesses**
    - *After my own family member criticized my gift as the work of a "Jezebel".*
- [ ] **Talking About Money**
    - *After being robbed by "so-called friends" that I allowed to stay in my home.*
- [ ] **Living in My Car or Motels**
    - *After being kicked out by my Sister & then Cousin's apartments.*
- [ ] **My Voice**
    - *After being stripped from my Godfather's church as a kid, because my parents divorced.*
- [ ] **My Thoughts**
    - *After experiencing my 1st suicide attempt 16 & pregnant.*
- [ ] **Being in Same-Sex Relationships**
    - *After my Aunt deemed me a "sinner" on her prayer wall.*
- [ ] **My Words and Writing**
    - *After someone criticized my intellectual creativity.*
- [ ] **My Inner Power**
    - *After a "so-called friend" told me she was jealous of my Spiritual Development.*

DEFENSE MECHANISMS: SHAME

Oftentimes we question as well as limit ourselves from spaces we hold on this Earth. We circle on this merry-go-round searching for something, anything to mask our true inner fears, uplift our feelings, as well as complete our worth. Being in such a lowly state of self-identification had me divert all outlets for speaking up for SELF & utilizing my inner voice as creativity. With this emotional imbalance, my self-awareness became oblivious & subjected to mental & physical abuse from my relationships with so-called friends, partners, even family.

We may also fear self-acceptance and put ourselves in positions or spaces in which we aren't always authentic with who we are CREATED to be. Portraying a false model of how we are living day to day life.

You may find yourself over-explaining, overspending, overtalking or overcompensating on a merry-go-round of not-truths to mask our natured truth with nurtured disempowerment.

PRETTY DAMN EXHAUSTING RIGHT!!

DEFENSE MECHANISMS: SHAME

We have the ability to GROW, LEARN & EVOLVE daily...

Through such experiences as noted above here's what I CHOOSE to grow through as wisdom:

- [ ] **My Body**
    - *I honor my body through a wealthy self-image & heart-filled mindset!*
- [ ] **My Natural Hair**
    - *I experience playful & exciting ways to enjoy my natural strands!*
- [ ] **Being Homeless**
    - *I value my space & sanctuary as HOME is where my heart is!*
- [ ] **My Crooked Smile**
    - *My smile is beautiful & bright and I will not dim my light to illuminate another!*
- [ ] **My Businesses**
    - *My work is good & how others perceive me is NOT my business!*
- [ ] **Talking About Money**
    - *I affirm that I am a wealthy Spirit... Mind, Body & Soul!*
- [ ] **Living in My Car or Motels**
    - *Wealth is a mindset & I declare beneficial abundance in ALL THINGS!*
- [ ] **My Voice**
    - *I create harmony through my words of power, whether written or spoken!*
- [ ] **My Thoughts**
    - *I am present with Source energy & radiate a subconscious mind as uplifting affirmations!*
- [ ] **Being in Same-Sex Relationships**
    - *I am LOVE, therefore I see love in ALL THINGS! I am never ashamed of my love...*
- [ ] **My Words and Writing**
    - *Known or unknown, I speak through my Higher Self with grace for ALL that resonate!*
- [ ] **My Inner Power**
    - *I accept my life's path as a Divine Vessel of LIGHT, LOVE, JOY & PEACE!*

DEFENSE MECHANISMS: SHAME

GOAL: Uproot shame with SELF-ID & CREATIVITY.

ASK YOURSELF - What AM I afraid to see when I look at myself in the mirror?

- [ ]
- [ ]
- [ ]
- [ ]
- [ ]
- [ ]
- [ ]
- [ ]

DEFENSE MECHANISMS: SHAME

EXERCISE: Reclaim your power within through self-awareness & creative opportunities.

GOAL:
- [ ] Dive into what you love with joy & fearlessness.

ASK YOURSELF - If I could direct a hollywood movie about my life's story, it would be called _____. Use this exercise to examine the main characters, the cast, the song for opening & ending credits. As well as your movie's MAIN theme song. BE as creative as possible, as we are ALWAYS manifesting!

DEFENSE MECHANISMS: SHAME

THE EARTH ANGEL'S HEALING GUIDE:

DEFENSE MECHANISMS: SELF-DOUBT

WORLDLY PROBLEMS. COSMIC SOLUTIONS!

DEFENSE MECHANISMS: SELF-DOUBT

Life has a funny way of showing:
- The Assignment vs The Purpose
- Divine Truth vs What We Tell Ourselves To Cope
- Valuable Lessons Through Chaos
- How To Create Happiness, Inside Out
- Where Peace Resides... As Mindfulness Within

My nephew called me today and the convo we had is one that I've had to have with myself in the mirror a MILLION times.

Being a young man of such integrity & amazing potential, through his tears and frustration of being a teenage father we managed to acknowledge all the above with a moment of INNER-standing. Together we experienced transmutation of INNERGY as someone he loves & values chose to just shut up, listen to & value him!

INNER-Standing, something these young folks truly need...

I listened to him.
Related to him.
And I highlighted his true nature as King.
Creating a safe space for him to INNER-stand his own truth.

I then shared a snippet of my story. A chapter out my book of life when I was selfish, fearful, insecure, unaware of my own identity & blinded by society.

I found myself mistrusting other people's opinions & doing dumb shit like:
- Being unsafe & sexually explicit.
- Dating gang members.
- Selling drugs.
- Driving intoxicated.
- Sneaking contraband in/out county jail visits.

I shared my story about how I risked being a Mom to my daughter, an Auntie to him, a nurse supporting others, a sister, a daughter, my sanity & my damn FREEDOM because I was so UNALIGNED with God's Light & Purpose. I became too damn focused on my own agenda of being "a somebody" to anybody.

I was holding down people that I know weren't loyal to me, that never uplifted me. I shared how I misdirected my energy as a soul vulture. And that vulture was the darkness of my ego.

Letting that shit go was one of the life altering decisions I made early on.
Yet I lacked consistency...

DEFENSE MECHANISMS: SELF-DOUBT

Approximately ten years ago, I experienced one of the lowest points of my life in which I didn't just think I was good enough for anything, I felt as if I wasn't good enough in ALL THINGS. At one point I was so numb that I believed there was nothing more to come of me, no confidence, no value, no energy, no mission. Not even being a mother to my child gave me purpose and I thought she'd be better off without me.

I inner-stood how he felt in this moment.

This illusion of unworthiness...

And just as I needed to remind myself then, I reminded my nephew now that...

We are reborn ungrounded souls. If we allow circumstances to attack us mentally, physically, emotionally and spiritually; It will drastically create a karmic pattern until we've granted our Soul permission to learn & accept THE LESSON.

> **We got to ask ourselves,**
> **"What is this teaching me?"**
> **AND**
> **"What am I willing to learn from this experience?"**

The negatives we tell ourselves become life hindering blockages & beliefs. <u>ONLY</u> if we allow them to.

Consistency is hard AF, yet it's a key ingredient to developing true oneness. As I remembered then, he'll remember now the importance of remaining faithful to wholeheartedly loving ourselves, to living in truth, removing self-created blockages & opening up to aligning with our soul's mission. It takes a great mental <u>S.H.I.F.T</u> to continuously recognize as well as acknowledge those dark trivial moments in the rabbit hole as an experience of <u>WISDOM</u>. We have to be consistent with reprogramming the mind to eliminate self doubt with positive actions. Ultimately embracing the seeds of essential growth that's needed to obtain the flow of our universal blessings.

✨✨✨ **#OnlyShiftWisdom** ✨✨✨

DEFENSE MECHANISMS: SELF-DOUBT

GOAL: Uproot self-doubt with the full potential of SELF-EXPLORATION.

ASK YOURSELF - On a scale of 1 to 10, how "In Control" of my life do I feel... RIGHT NOW?!
1 - 2 - 3 - 4 - 5 - 6 - 7 - 8 - 9 - 10
If you are not at a 10, place you hands over your heart then ask your Higher Self
"What Do I Require To Align At A TEN?"

☐

☐

☐

☐

☐

☐

☐

☐

DEFENSE MECHANISMS: SELF-DOUBT

EXERCISE: "I AM" the INNER POWER, required to overcome.

GOAL: Determines how you may punish the SELF consciously or unconsciously?

ASK YOURSELF - How can I release resistance & self-loathing with acknowledging (1) fear & (1) affirmation... Allow the self to experience ONENESS with dissolution.

Write out a (-) experience, fold the paper counterclockwise 3x(s) & then BURN in a fire safe container to release!

Write out a (+) experience OR affirmation to embody. Call this into your BE-ing, fold the paper clockwise 3x(s) & keep this reminder with you to read aloud in a mirror DAILY for a minimum of 21 days.

_____

_____

_____

_____

_____

_____

_____

_____

_____

_____

_____

_____

_____

_____

_____

_____

DEFENSE MECHANISMS: SELF-DOUBT

THE EARTH ANGEL'S HEALING GUIDE:

DEFENSE MECHANISMS: GRIEF

WORLDLY PROBLEMS. COSMIC SOLUTIONS!

DEFENSE MECHANISMS: GRIEF

Yes! It is hella hard to experience love once again when you've felt as if you've lost the person you love THE MOST in death. Unhealed grief can take you on a vengeance. A rage against the self as well as others to the point where you just want to "kill" any & everything moving... INCLUDING YOURSELF.

How scary is it to traumatically worry endlessly over circumstances you cannot control, yet are destined to experience. Afterall, we were all once reborn from death as the rebirth of our soul's mission. Whether you believe in reincarnation and past lives or not, one thing is for sure with two things for certain...
- SHIFT Happens!
- And we are LOVE

The Bible states that we were all born in sin.
I tend to focus on my "Spiritual Relationship" within, through the Light of God!

For me, that means as a Spirit having a human experience we are created through God's image of Divine Love to fulfill our assignment as compassionate love. Focusing on living in this world vs being of this world & subjecting our experiences negatively to the chaos. As love, we are then required to intentionally RELEASE those parts of ourselves that cause trauma, misconception & circumstances of societal hindrance. Words will not always express how to move through this alignment, therefore we become guided by our experiences & how spaces or people make us FEEL.

Through release we make space for opportunities to EXPERIENCE remembrance and the equity of peace as well as understanding. We get to choose unique evolution daily, the same energy that turned a dark Universe into the Light of our days.

I could've had five kids by the time I was twenty-one. Hell to be completely honest, had I listened to the BS of others in my family... My daughter wouldn't be here.

Truth is, my first miscarriage was just eight weeks after my daughter was born, YES eight weeks. I was sixteen still having unprotected sex, with unhealed stitches just four weeks after giving birth.

Because my relationship at the time was emotionally young, mentally frustrating & physically abusive... The stress and tension became too overwhelming for my youthfulness, that my mind & body rejected carrying another child. My first pregnancy was my body & my choice, whereas the second was a surprise interruption... That I was grateful for. I did not want to bring another child into such a chaotic space.

Thereafter my first two pregnancies, I experienced my third pregnancy & first abortion... For many of the same reasons. Here I am now seventeen, a senior in high school with a seven month old baby, who was forcing herself to walk. Mommabear's intuition knew she was attempting to move out the way for "something" & yes, when she asked I told her that I was pregnant yet again.

DEFENSE MECHANISMS: GRIEF

Being in the same tumultuously draining relationship, this time it was my decision to have some sorta control over my life.

I asked Mommabear to catch the bus with me to Atlantic City as I chose to terminate my pregnancy of three and a half months.

Mommabear kept asking me the entire bus ride if I was truly sure because the public ugly cry was just not giving. Realizing I lacked self-control, through tears of guilt & sorrow I felt as if I was doing the right thing. The grief of losing a child is one thing, compared to taking life away.

For a short few years, I held onto this incestant mourning wondering if I could ever have kids again. Then sure enough, at nineteen I terminated my fourth pregnancy.

After kicking out my ex & watching me start a new job with a busted lip, my neighbor (we'll call him King Tutt) at the time became a sounding board for me. I'm not quite sure how our late night smoke sessions & soul talks turned into a sexual relationship, yet it did. And because he had a live-in girlfriend, I damn sure wasn't about to bring a baby into another love triangle. Although he asked to go with me, I found myself back on the bus to AC… ALONE to terminate another life.

"Never again. Never again. Never again." - That's what I kept telling myself.

I lied to myself because now my ass was twenty years old, head over heels with my best friend at the time's sibling. A seventeen year old fresh out of the juvenile detention center. This rollercoaster was a doozy from the door…

We chatted about Vanilla Cream a few chapters back & yes, I experienced my fifth pregnancy.

After experiencing this love at first sight and empowering type of connection, this situationship became stagnant and confusing real quick. I spent more nights trying not to regret my love than days actually enjoying or feeling loved. When Vanilla Cream told me that their ex-girlfriend (who was trying to get him back) said she hoped our child didn't look like a dinosaur like my daughter… I blacked out!

First and foremost I knew it was pure jealousy due to the fact that I was pregnant and not her, yet I was grateful to know that his sneaky ass had been talking behind my back to her sneaky ass. I immediately didn't care about carrying a child anymore & I wanted to FIGHT. Not over some nigga tho, I wanted to drag this chick because not onl did you disrespect my unborn, you disrespected my daughter.

So yes, I made him bring her to me and dragging her ass through Regency East Apartments is exactly what I did. I would've been in jail from bashing her head into the concrete if it wasn't for him pulling me

DEFENSE MECHANISMS: GRIEF

off her. And just like a weak bitch, as soon as I was up & let her skull loose, she kicked me… Right in my stomach.

This chapter is hard for me to write because I truly wanted to be in love with this person.
I wanted to forever feel as safe and secure as I did when we first met in that driveway.
I wanted to experience growth, new experiences & fresh opportunities.
I wanted to expand my family.
I wanted to give birth to my son.

After the fight, I went to my cousin's apartment & my uterus was throbbing.
I thought I had to pee really bad & the pain was from holding my bladder for so long.

When I got up from the toilet, it was filled with huge blood clots & my fetus was still attached to a dangling cord.

I was so fucking angry that I allowed these people,
BOTH *him & her to get me in a position where I am yet again grieving over another loss.*

Before flushing my unborn child down the toilet, being super petty I texted him a picture saying "I hope you're happy now, cause we just lost our son!"

I haven't looked at my body, relationships nor being a Mom quite the same… It took me until my late twenties & early thirties to begin reclaiming my power with no regrets from ALL that I've experienced with birth, death and rebirth.

Day by day I struggled to love myself and it taught me to highlight my quirks as uniqueness.
I struggled to believe I was loved and this taught me that I am deserving of love as I AM LOVE.
I struggled with creativity and I chose to illuminate agony with the ingenuity of my words.
I struggled to live, live fulfilled and this granted me grace to appreciate the vitality of the breath.
I struggled with aspiration & purpose, this confronted as well as blessed fancying TRUE Freedom.

DEFENSE MECHANISMS: GRIEF

In the midst of these karmic cycles & although it took ten plus years to appreciate;
I take away with me a few things:

- **SHIFT Happens!**
    - The trajectory of pain & controversy was given to experience as a resource. A tool to see past the surface of bitter ends and into the awakening of creation. Who would think that such negative circumstances with life & death, would grant me access to higher perspectives of personal & sensual transformation inside out.
- **I AM LOVE**
    - I am no longer afraid of loving myself, my sexuality, being in love or distributing compassion to others. I lean into the knowing that if I am created from love, I permeate Divine Love. This allows me to fill my own cup with self-mastery, self-care, self-love & wholesomely appreciate ALL that I Am as God as God is ALL that I Am. I choose to create space, even through turmoil to cherish self-honoring purification.

Through such a path with my womb, I've been able to reflect as well as amplify my vision of being a Mother. This includes how I encourage my daughter to BE. Be the best version of herself to her Higher Self! Encouraging the responsibility to love & care for the mind, body & especially spirit.

I am forever grateful for the losses.
As they have matured my outlook on being a different type of parent.
Creating different kinds of experiences.
Being in a different space of consciousness.
Creating a different level of love and joy.
Being a different kind of woman.

DEFENSE MECHANISMS: GRIEF

GOAL: Uproot grief with GRATITUDE.

ASK YOURSELF - Where have I experienced loss or excessive adversity?

- [ ]
- [ ]
- [ ]
- [ ]
- [ ]
- [ ]
- [ ]
- [ ]

DEFENSE MECHANISMS: GRIEF

EXERCISE: There's Gratitude In Solitude!

GOAL:
☐ Analyze the expansion of thought patterns, while spending exclusive time in meditation.

ASK YOURSELF - What stagnant energy am I experiencing in my life? What repetitive cycles do I now notice? Take 15 minutes a day for the next several days & rediscover your truth through self-actualization. How can I recreate my experiences in a way that EMPOWERS growth as well as self-love?

_____

_____

_____

_____

_____

_____

_____

_____

_____

_____

_____

_____

_____

_____

_____

_____

_____

_____

_____

_____

DEFENSE MECHANISMS: GRIEF

THE EARTH ANGEL'S HEALING GUIDE:

DEFENSE MECHANISMS: FEAR

WORLDLY PROBLEMS, COSMIC SOLUTIONS!

DEFENSE MECHANISMS: FEAR

The manipulation of fear is the hardest part of self-healing. While yearning to remain consistent with restoration, we overcome alarming apprehension through the power of benevolent LOVE.

A love that may only create Divine compassion & joy.

Every time we are challenged with a new form of manipulation, we are challenged to renew our frequency with our spiritual tools and resources to align with a warm heart as well as tranquil unity.

Fear can manifest as the depiction of confusion, chaos, anger and ....
DISTRACTIONS!

Let's take a look at the concept of - Delusion VS Disillusion:

> If we take a look at the ***illusions or delusions*** of our experiences, we'll find that what we were "taught" promotes fear. Versus the power to accept how we choose to learn & relate within our unique relationship with God.
>
> The illusion is we exist the way we are taught. Taught by our parents, our relationships, experiences, conversations, media and the reflection society portrays onto us (outside in).
>
> We are taught to depict our existence as a hustle, hunger, confusion, hierarchy and end up hating ourselves as well as others that do not conform to the subconscious way of thinking & believing. Through hidden agendas, barriers and lack of trust we counter-react rather than respond earnestly to the lies, frustration or DISTRACTIONS…
>
> Disease is often an illusion of the mind & body. Medicinal infiltration of our DNA, our birthright.
> With vaccinations, prescriptions, fast food and pandemics; we are exploited to exist within by-laws or workarounds that do not support our healing in humanity. In Buddhism, this is known as Samsara - "The Great Deceiver"; unprecedented forms of repeated karmic cycles misleading birth, trauma, drama, death and misery.
>
>> It is as if we aren't worthy of truth.
>> ***TRUTH IS, Mother Nature heals!***

DEFENSE MECHANISMS: FEAR

Disillusion however is a MINDSET. The perception we create with higher learning & faith through our experiences. Through delusions of society, we have the ability to awaken unto our "Divine Mind'. We can begin to honor our relationship with Christ Consciousness to know, believe & trust that...

There is NO SEPARATION from God, if we CHOOSE to see God in ALL THINGS!

Created with an INNER-standing of balance & wisdom, we elucidate transformation & truth with the Spirit of Self as well as the enlightenment of the ego. The resolution is mindfulness for the evolution of spiritual growth:

- [ ] Healthy eating habits & natural living. To cleanse the mind as well as the body, making room to receive more of what you desire.
- [ ] Codes of communication. Angel numbers & guides, planetary signs, ancient symbols, divination messages that guide you to make the BEST decisions with confidence & integrity..
- [ ] Reading more to teach yourself as well as others. Applying wisdom into self, friends, family and communities that fuel your body & soul's mission.
- [ ] Meditation. Protecting & transforming energy as well as owning the alchemist within you!

Disillusion is the process of intentional deconditioning capital or conformed thoughts, behaviors & actions. There is no reason we shouldn't be able to LIVE FREE. A life of joy!

As I mentioned above, Mother Earth heals. We experience Earth's natural gems by entering a state of relaxation and peace. The innate state of peace is when the mind grants the body permission to rest. Rest to receive transparency for self-guidance. Leadership to support our goals, dreams & vision. Protection that repels toxic energy & attracts united relationships.

Using enhancements such as crystals to connect with the frequencies of the Earth's core. Bridging meals and vitamin supplements with herbs, organic fruits & veggies to sustain natural energy within the body. Conjuring sublingual or topical oils to balance the equilibriums of vital cells. Aligning the grace of silence to audaciously invigorate sacred healing and fulfillment.

With all that is always available to us NATURALLY, why would we lie dormant in the illusion?

It's time we as a collective awaken the Spirit, <u>in Spirit</u> & rise to POWER!

DEFENSE MECHANISMS: FEAR

Learn To Call Back Your Power!

As we watch worldly, societal or political views and events via uproar; I often wonder where's the uprising of our innate culture? Spiritual revolution?

Let's consider the advice you gave your younger self.

.

.

Having a human experience is forever interchangeable & evolving…
Therefore as a Spiritual BE-ing, inner work is a MUST!
As through our own experiences we CREATE the life we love in wisdom!

It's important to recall the soul's mission DAILY!

Do not allow the self to be distracted by the false Gods, the views of the world. Instead CHOOSE to focus on one's generational healing. Intuitively transcending multi-generational triggers and rhymes of unhealthy belief systems. Take some time to channel energy into rejuvenating your bloodline.

Reestablishing wisdom of your lifestyle..
Reclaiming love with compassion & forgiveness..
Recreating joy for all that excites you..
Remembering wealth as a mindset.
Rejuvenating health that radiates vitality.
Replenishing capital for the purity of agriculture & the planet.
Restructuring prosperity through investments & purchasing land.
Refocusing on stocks to enhance economic value.
Reiterating savvy knowledge to reconstruct businesses.

CHOOSING TO BE.

Be conscious & forthcoming with what you feed the Spirit and your INNERGY to sustain positive vibrations across all time, places, people & dimensions you hold for.

DEFENSE MECHANISMS: FEAR

"Your tears are pre-registered for JOY"!

Cleanse ALL the DEEPEST, MOST VULNERABLE, yet VALUABLE spaces of time that I have EVER encountered.
.
.
.

We are reminded that although we are subjected to trauma and pain...
We have the opportunity to be a witness & testimony to this MF'n healing too & that's what is best to choose! Sharing truth with grace because "pain" only lingers if you allow it to... The trauma was not ours to carry nor aligned to weigh the soul down.

It's within the gratitude & creativity of our story, that we may IF EVER spread ourselves on a "cross" (from the North, South, East and West) across all planes.

I invite you to HONOR the journey and ONLY leave with the grace and PEACE that you choose to create NOW............... TODAY!

In the present...
Moment by moment...

True healing is not in the absence of pain or dis-ease.
Yet in the PRESENCE and POWER of
Faith, **E**nlightenment, **A**dventure and **R**eorientation with our spirituality!

DEFENSE MECHANISMS: FEAR

Divination Message: March 2021

REST IN POWER - Before you go to sleep… Affirm, Declare and Decree,

.
.

"As I rest in power, I am no longer attached to any spiritual attachments, entities or energies. I release any malignant energy that no longer serves my divine highest consciousness. I call forward my ancestors of benevolence and sovereignty as my shield of divine light & protection serving unto my elevated good!

Asè Asè Asè"

.
.

RISE IN POWER - When you wake up… Affirm, Declare and Decree,

.
.

"I rise in power, cloaked, guided and protected by ancestors, archangels and spirit guides to start my day in/with...

(set your DAILY intentions)

As I rise within my divine light, I command & call back all my energy & power to my vessel 10x fold serving me with nothing but beneficial energy, mind, body, spirit and essence unto my elevated good!"

~ **Novah's Son**

DEFENSE MECHANISMS: FEAR

GOAL: Uproot fear with ONENESS.

ASK YOURSELF - What have been the greatest fears that restricted my way of thinking, believing & doing & WHY? Recall moments you accepted limitations & decide to CHOOSE a different outcome.

- [ ]
- [ ]
- [ ]
- [ ]
- [ ]
- [ ]
- [ ]
- [ ]

DEFENSE MECHANISMS: FEAR

EXERCISE: My life in trivia.

GOAL:

- [ ] Regift your LIGHT BODY to the soul with new opportunities, experiences & mindfulness.

ASK YOURSELF - What are my "Go To" favorites & choices that bring the BEST version of myself to the world? If you do not currently have or do something listed ……….. CREATE IT - DREAM BIG!

CURRENT RESIDENCE:
_____

OCCUPATION:
_____

PET:
_____

BREAKFAST:
_____

BAR:
_____

CLOTHING:
_____

SPA:
_____

CAR:
_____

DREAM JOB:
_____

COMFORT FOOD:
_____

HOBBY:
_____

DEFENSE MECHANISMS: FEAR

PASTIME:

POLITICAL PARTY:

CHARITY:

MAIN COURSE:

DESSERT:

DRINK:

ZODIAC SIGN:

OUTDOOR ACTIVITY:

SHOES:

GAME:

SPORT:

WEBSITE:

TV PROGRAM:

RESTAURANT:

THE EARTH ANGEL'S HEALING GUIDE:

FORGIVENESS

WORLDLY PROBLEMS. COSMIC SOLUTIONS!

FORGIVENESS

Feeling like an outcast in my family as well as like I do not belong on this Earth gave me motivation & strength to leave. Moving to Minnesota was the beginning of my fresh start. I had a stable job, a fiancè, what I considered to be a family unit & I FINALLY decided to enroll in a nursing program to obtain my Bachelor's degree.

While working part-time as a transporter at St. Joseph's Hospital, I'm getting off the elevator returning a patient's bed to their room and my phone rings. Chocolate was calling.

We hadn't spoken in a calm, cool, collected way in years due to the toxic relationship I ended by putting his clothes outside & locking him out for putting his hands in me. AND fathering twin girls outside of our relationship. However, this phone call felt like it would be different, so I answered; and at first I just listened.

"Shavon, I know our back & forth relationship or lack thereof over the past 10 or so years has not been the best & I did a lot of shit that I am not proud of as a man. I mean, you did your shit too, but I'm not calling you to blame or shame you because I know we were BOTH young & dumb. I take FULL responsibility for my actions, what I did to us, what I did to you as well as what I didn't do for you or my daughter.

.

.

I never want you to hate me or for me not to be a part of your life and our daughter's life. You've been raising her by yourself and I truly thank you & applaud you from the bottom of my heart for being the best mom to our baby. I have not always shown you the respect you deserve but I love you, you're my daughter's mom & I just pray every night to God that you can forgive me."

Chocolate proceeded to acknowledge me for all that I AM.
As a human.
As a spiritual being.
As a mom.
As a woman.
And it was that very conversation that healed our relationship to co-parent.

It was vital for me to let him know how I was feeling.

FORGIVENESS

"I hear you and I need you to know that I have already forgiven you as well as MYSELF.

You're absolutely right, we were BOTH young & ignorant to what it takes to sustain a healthy as well as stable relationship. You know I grew up without having my Dad, a protector in my life. One minute, I was Daddy's Princess & the next second he was gone. And still to this day, I do not have a healthy outlook of nor relationship with him.

I do not want my daughter to experience that!

I love you as my daughter's Dad & despite what we've been through, I have NEVER spoken ill about you or against you in her presence. That was something I experienced and it hurt me then to hear someone speaking about death or toxicity over my Dad, because that made me see him in a different light.

I never want my daughter to hear negativity about you.
I never want her to have this false perception of men.
I never want her to experience you in any way, other than being her protector.

I thank you for calling me and sharing this moment with me, but I learned to forgive you years ago.
I do not hate you, I can not hate you.
I am proud of the man you have chosen to be!"

This moment of clarity enhanced a blessing for our souls for healing & restoration.

Put us in a room together today and you would never know about the toxic relationship we experienced together. My daughter still does not know or may never know of our past relationship, because with moving forward, we chose to keep that destructiveness in the past!

We are not just co-parents, we are truly a BLENDED FAMILY.

We want our daughter, actually ALL KIDS involved to experience love, unity, trust, resilience & communication as ONE FAMILY when it comes to their upbringing. Something neither Chocolate nor I had a chance to experience growing up.

FORGIVENESS

Forgiveness of <u>SELF</u> is necessary to journey forward …………………….. PERIOD!
Forgiveness is the doorway to self-healing.

With HEALING.
With PEACE.
With GRATITUDE.
With GRACE.
With ENERGY.
With HONESTY.
With INTEGRITY.
With WHOLENESS.
With ONENESS.
With STRENGTH.
With RESILIENCE.
With BALANCE.
SELF-MASTERY.
& SELF-LOVE!

Forgiveness is not for anyone else… It's to REBUILD within you.
      1 - For being out of alignment with your purpose.
      2 - For being out of alignment with your peace of mind!
      3 - For being out of alignment with your vision.

Move FORWARD in the foundation, knowing it's ok to acknowledge where we once were.
Yet we are required to water the wisdom of our experiences for growth & evolution…

We are seeds planting new energy.
Enlightenment DAILY!
Growing in light & love.

We're sprouting, as we are lit by the SUN.
Therefore we must not diminish because of faults & baggage.
Nor perish due to outside noise.

As we choose to remove ALL LAYERS… There's an opportunity to get to the root & **<u>UPROOT</u>**!
- Applying nurture where it's needed…
- Hydrate where you may be replenished…
- Heal what is meant to be youthful…
- And create revolution inside out, as you should…

FORGIVENESS

No one can judge you as our mind can ONLY believe what we CHOOSE to accept!

If we feel an energetic pull of negativity, know that somewhere in your timeline you're allowing it & one can only judge themselves as they judge you! Mirroring. Self-reflecting. As we are one & were once where one another has been.

No one is absolutely perfect, yet perfectly CREATED for your soul mission!

FORGIVENESS

Divination Message: July 2021

For the next 7 days…

💙 Envision a BLUE aura of compassion encircling you in a counter-clockwise rotation. Releasing all that no longer serves you in hurt, anger, frustration, trauma or pain.

💚 Then simultaneously usher in a clockwise GREEN aura of light for healing, growth & protection swarming around you. Hugging you. Embracing you. Enriching the energy of your higher SELF that holds you.

Uplifting your vibration & Spirit!
Across ALL time, spaces, places, people and dimensions.

💛 On day 7, light a YELLOW candle for the audacity & willpower to illuminate every aspect of your life in a loving peace & grace a loved one or an ancestor of benevolence with the same energy, one in the same.

- - - - - - - - -

☀️ EMBODY THE SPIRIT OF S.H.I.F.T
(Spirit, Healing, Intuition, Freedom & Truth)

WITHIN YOU!

FORGIVENESS

EXERCISE: Release judgment. Ritual mindfulness to enhance forgiveness for ALL involved.

GOAL:

☐ Diminish your burdens & release that which no longer serves you!

ASK YOURSELF - List the #1 thing that you DISLIKE or have the MOST difficulty dealing with about a person. *Now write out a time in which **YOU** did the EXACT thing or possessed a similar character trait.*

FORGIVENESS

THE EARTH ANGEL'S HEALING GUIDE:

INTIMACY

WORLDLY PROBLEMS. COSMIC SOLUTIONS!

INTIMACY

"Into Me Eye See"

How can we APPLY the wisdom of our emotional balance?

The truth is… TRUTH is often still and it's not until we are patient enough with ourselves that we choose to rest & listen to the depth as well as whispers of our divine truth within.

It is not until we see ourselves AS TRUTH, that we begin to truly SEE into the seat of our soul.

I am remembering who I AM as the true Divine Light BE-ing that God created me to be versus suffering in all that was designed to keep me in bondage or karmic generational loops.

GRATITUDE is one of the highest, elevated psyches aligned with evolution & manifestation.

Amidst the passing of my mother in August 2020,
I had subconsciously avoided celebrating anything, especially any holidays after her funeral.
I assumed my strength required me to extend my gifts beyond emotional capacity.
I put off grieving not only to honor her, but to be of strength for others.

Yet, she was MY MOM!

I had lost someone that I loved in physical form.
I noticed that I had been unintentionally focusing on the what was only temporarily lost,
rather than become reminded of all that I had gained with spiritual transparency.

This past holiday season 2021, I found myself allocating my energy 50/50.

I surrounded my BE-ing with loved ones in New Jersey for Thanksgiving.
Absorbing infectious laughter during my Gaga's 90th Birthday celebration.
Reflecting on cherished memories, going through OLD ass childhood photos.
As well as embraced an "impetuous love interest", despite residual fears & hidden triggers.

December 2021, I snuggled in.
Hibernating through the Minnesota snow showers.
Experiencing a level of gratitude that allowed me to simply melt.

I gave myself what I had been needing in August.
I shifted into a divine appreciation for the PRESENT.

INTIMACY

I chose to seclude myself from social media & society including clients.
I chose to fast, consuming only hydrating fruits & vegetables as well as drinking water or tea.
I chose to rest, turning off all 10 of my daily alarms.
I allowed my Spirit to rise in solace.

AND I watched ONLY Christmas themed movies, at least three a day or NO TV at all.

I created a conscious connection into the depth of divine compassion,
I chose to give myself MORE of what I once sought after from others as well as amongst
"materialism":

Enhanced PATIENCE.
Deeper GRACE.
Extended STILLNESS.
Additional REJUVENATION.
Enriched CLARITY.
Radiated CREATIVITY.

Above All Else,
Universal LOVE.

I captivated my sovereignty by acknowledging all that
I am intangibly indebted to within, as PEACE OF MIND.

As you dive into your journey, BE INTIMATE with you.
Channel your sacred gratitude for the present.
Exemplify with fulfillment the genuinity of your soul's needs & heart's desires.

Transcend into your ascension and ground into your soul mission.

I AM READY MEDITATION

Place your hands over your heart.
Left palm over heart space, right over left.

Under the dawn of the glistening skies, envision yourself outside in a grassy field.
Feel the glow of the divine Moon shadowing over your vessel
& illuminating the authority of your soul within.

Notice in the middle of the field, there's a HUGE Rowan Tree
as it whispers your name & instructs you to "*Sit With Me*"!

As you walk towards the tree you embrace the grounding of Mother Earth
beneath your feet & in the midst of the wild between your toes.

Take a seat at the roots, by the soul of the tree.
(with your eyes closed, look up toward the center of your brows).

Invite Universal & Source energy to align with your center.
Visualize a bright white light,
beaming through your crown directly into your Heart Chakra.

Speak your intentions to the Earth...

Using the palms of your hands, vibrationally ignite
& push a green energy ball fulfilled with your intention
from your Heart Chakra into the roots of the tree.

When you feel it, take a deep breath & affirm,
"I AM READY TO RECEIVE"!

Feel your wings of oneness & fulfillment grow strong
from the depth of your shoulder blades as courage within.

Now envision your spirit team of ancestors, ascended masters, archangels and guides
standing to your left & right. Know that your support team is with you.

Release your intent with confidence, protection, healing, grace, joy, peace & pure bliss!.

NOW FLYYYYYY! SOAR. & TRUST that your soul knows to lead the way!

I AM READY MEDITATION

Energetically bring yourself back down.
Wiggle your toes & fingers.
Ground into the present moment.

Take 3 deep breaths!
Full inhales. Full exhales.

Recite Grounding Chant. (pg. 34)

INTIMACY

EXERCISE: Into me, eye see.

GOAL:
☐ Be honest with yourself rather than being judgemental.

ASK YOURSELF - You judge people, we all do. How about judging The Self for a change. Ask yourself... How do I judge myself? How do I view major aspects of who I AM? Rate the contributions of your mindset 1 to 10, then choose how you may enhance it!

HONESTY: **1 - 2 - 3 - 4 - 5 - 6 - 7 - 8 - 9 - 10**

_____

GENEROSITY: **1 - 2 - 3 - 4 - 5 - 6 - 7 - 8 - 9 - 10**

_____

FORGIVENESS: **1 - 2 - 3 - 4 - 5 - 6 - 7 - 8 - 9 - 10**

_____

HAPPINESS: **1 - 2 - 3 - 4 - 5 - 6 - 7 - 8 - 9 - 10**

_____

LOYALTY: **1 - 2 - 3 - 4 - 5 - 6 - 7 - 8 - 9 - 10**

_____

UNIQUENESS: **1 - 2 - 3 - 4 - 5 - 6 - 7 - 8 - 9 - 10**

_____

HUMOR: **1 - 2 - 3 - 4 - 5 - 6 - 7 - 8 - 9 - 10**

_____

INTELLIGENCE: **1 - 2 - 3 - 4 - 5 - 6 - 7 - 8 - 9 - 10**

_____

INTIMACY

ACCOMMODATING: **1 - 2 - 3 - 4 - 5 - 6 - 7 - 8 - 9 - 10**

TALENTED: **1 - 2 - 3 - 4 - 5 - 6 - 7 - 8 - 9 - 10**

CONFIDENCE: **1 - 2 - 3 - 4 - 5 - 6 - 7 - 8 - 9 - 10**

HUMBLENESS: **1 - 2 - 3 - 4 - 5 - 6 - 7 - 8 - 9 - 10**

LOVING: **1 - 2 - 3 - 4 - 5 - 6 - 7 - 8 - 9 - 10**

TOLERANCE: **1 - 2 - 3 - 4 - 5 - 6 - 7 - 8 - 9 - 10**

SPONTANEITY: **1 - 2 - 3 - 4 - 5 - 6 - 7 - 8 - 9 - 10**

HEALTH: **1 - 2 - 3 - 4 - 5 - 6 - 7 - 8 - 9 - 10**

CREATIVITY: **1 - 2 - 3 - 4 - 5 - 6 - 7 - 8 - 9 - 10**

FASHIONABLE: **1 - 2 - 3 - 4 - 5 - 6 - 7 - 8 - 9 - 10**

ALIGNMENT AFFIRMATIONS

Divination Message: March 2021

"I AM safe, as I AM cloaked & grounded.

I AM grounded, as I invoke confidence!

I AM confident, as I AM creative.

I create, as I invoke the fullness of joy.

I present joy, as I maintain my inner strength.

I AM strong, as I transform my capabilities.

I AM willing & capable, as I choose love.

I choose to love, as I AM loved.

I AM love, as I AM free to express my truth.

I AM truth, as I remain calm.

I AM calm, as I find positive resolution.

I AM absolute, as I define my connections.

I facilitate & connect, as I cultivate peace ... within.

I AM peace, as I AM of Faithful Sense.

I AM the Omniscient of Grace & Ease."

~ **Novah's Son**

THE EARTH ANGEL'S HEALING GUIDE:

WILLPOWER

WORLDLY PROBLEMS. COSMIC SOLUTIONS!

WILLPOWER

January 6th, 2021 what I thought would be a normal, fun day with me and my Sunshine, turned into a straight up shit show.

In my Spirit I felt my baby's energy dwindling & she was no longer a baby anymore. I knew that she craved her individuality as well as independence. I also felt the grief she had repressed from the passing of her Nana. A woman she loved, respected, confided in about everything left us physically just six months prior. As her Mom, it was my overthinking as well as overprotective nature that caused all hell on Earth to break "through" in our 1300 square feet apartment.

We had been planning Sunshine's next steps after she graduated high school. She wanted to move back home to New Jersey and decided that she would be closer to her Nana, Dad & favorite cousin who is more like her brother.

Weeks before this decision, I sat at my ancestor's altar meditating and heard our loved one's across the veil say "Let her go, let her fly… We got her! And if her head so much as tilts in the opposite direction, we'll knock her shoulders straight. She ain't on that phone all day for nothing, we send her signs DAILY & she knows it! She pays attention!"

After this Divine message I enter her room and we have such a unique and gratifying conversation…

ME: "Do you meditate like I taught you and connect with your ancestors?"

SUNSHINE: "Yea… I don't always sit at the altar all the time but I mean I talk to them often. Why?"

ME: "Have you felt like they're connecting to you easier or more frequently lately?"

SUNSHINE: "Well whenever I think about something with school, my goals or if I'm manifesting, then I'll see something on Instagram or something on YouTube pop ups about it… And I noticed that when I'm sleeping I feel more at peace… protected."

ME: "That's good, I love that!"

SUNSHINE: "Why you asking?"

ME: "Well today, just now actually, I was meditating at the altar & heard them tell me *"Let her fly! We got her! And if her head so much as tilts in the opposite direction, we'll knock her shoulders straight. She ain't on that phone all day for nothing, we send her signs DAILY & she knows it! She pays attention!"*

SUNSHINE: (she looks up & with this sly grin) - "OMG! Why y'all telling her MY BUSINESSSSSS!"

WILLPOWER

We both laughed, I gave her a huge hug and kiss & it was THAT very moment... Mommabear had to let her Babybear grow into the beautiful, smart, creative young lady she was becoming.

ASK ME IF I LISTENED THO??!!

Notice that on January 6th, I mentioned "all hell breaks THROUGH", and NOT breaks loose.

Although it was the biggest argument we ever had that disrupted our household. The most abusive we had ever been to one another... verbally, emotionally & physically. This particular argument also became the catapult our soul's mission required, to experience a higher level of FORGIVENESS as well as WILLPOWER.

It took everything in me not to disrespect my daughter the way she had me.
It took the strength of Archangel Michael to keep me from disdain & shutting her out..
It took nothing but Divine healing to APPLY a higher level of self-discipline.
It took all forms of grace to instantly acknowledge wrongdoing & seek to rebuild.

After our fight that night, my immediate response was to
CLEANSE, CLEAR, RELEASE & PROTECT.

Although she called me toxic, cussed me out and pulled my hair; Then ran out of the house...

Instead of being filled with anger, disappointment or betrayal, I proceeded to purify & disentangle the negativity within the air. I walked through every corner, saging & chanting.

Calling forward my light within.
Calling forward her light within.
Calling forward effective communication.
Calling forward the angels of forgiveness.
Calling forward the will of God.
Calling forward balanced INNER-standing.
Calling forward Divine compassion.
Calling forward the love of the Spirit.

I then sat in my favorite sectional seat in the living room, by the ancestor's altar & called forward a platinum white light of healing and protection to envelop us.

Our bond as Mother and Daughter.
Our union as Spiritual BE-ings.
Our growth as Earth Angels.

WILLPOWER

While releasing any and all distress, I journeyed through self-reflection. I remembered the last time I ever raised my voice or spoke ill to my Mommabear. I recalled that July right before she passed, her confirmation to me that through the bickering & sarcasm, she loved me wholeheartedly and I was never considered a burden in her eyes. She reminded me that our bond was solely protective & her greatest fear was disconnecting from me as I grew into my own woman. Losing a love she never felt.

I realized in this moment with Sunshine, THIS WAS MY FEAR!
Yet I knew she would be safe...

The only phone call I made was to her Dad.
I let him know I would be flying her out to New Jersey a few months before we planned.

Inside out, I stopped fighting Sunshine's growth. It wasn't for me to contain, contrive, nor control. I released the burden felt & discontent repressed, when I learned to cultivate the essence of freedom!

About a month and a half later after our fight, I woke up at the crack of dawn to meditate. I felt this overwhelming urge that I needed to hug my daughter, to let her know, I missed her. I life her. I love her. And I forgive her... as well as myself!

Within just a few sacred minutes of meditation, I found my Spirit transported to her Dad's house and at the front door. Gliding straight into the room she shared with her bonus-sister, my Spirit watched her from the doorway resting on the right side of the bed by the window. I watched her peak an eye out the cover & then toss the covers over her head. Comforting back into a restful state.

I ushered to the bedside and was guided to perform a powerful Reiki session. Allowing my Spirit to place one hand over my heart and the other hand over her heart. I asked the Light & Will of God to send us elevated restoration so that we can move forward with the highest vibration of forgiveness & unconditional love.

I was positioned at her bedside until I heard "Your work is good, It is done!". I then released, closed the Reiki session with ABSOLUTE gratitude unto our oversouls, the angels and our benevolent ancestors. Then I returned my Spirit to my body.
Safe & sound in my own space, apartment and bed to rest.
Mindfully I became present with healing.

The next morning we talked for the first time through the argument and our discrepancies via Facetime. Sunshine told me she had an urge to call me the night before but thought I'd be asleep, since the east coast is two hours ahead of the midwest.

WILLPOWER

After we apologized to one another for being out of alignment, I started to tell her about the spiritual experience I had less than twenty-four hours ago and she stopped me...

ME: "Do you sleep on the right side of the bed?"

SUNSHINE: "Yea, I like to be by the window & door, in case I have to use the bathroom in the middle of the night. Yesterday morning was weird though."

ME: "Why is that, you couldn't sleep?"

SUNSHINE: "No Mommmm, I was half asleep yesterday morning but I felt like someone was watching me from our door. I thought it could've been my Dad, but the door was still closed. I just saw a shadow of light standing there."

ME: "Were you scared?"

SUNSHINE: "I mean NO. I looked out the covers & just layed back down. I just felt a sense of protection and that gave me peace to go back to sleep."

ME: "Wow! That was me. You saw me! Holy shit, you saw me! I knew we had a dope ass relationship but damn, you really felt & saw my energy travel to you."

I revealed the full cyclomatic meditation and Reiki energy healing that I experienced with her. And she gave me confirmation that we'd be

God had brought us THROUGH to mend karmic cycles & we did not resist.

WILLPOWER

EXERCISE: Knocks me off my feet!

GOAL:

☐ Provide yourself with INNER-standing…

ASK YOURSELF - Every now & then something occurs that will knock you off your feet! You may even feel like you're misunderstood. To gain INNER-standing, write a song that allows you to look into your soul. Use a combination of words & emotions that will gravitate to your soul. With growth, comes a rich & fulfilled life.

WILLPOWER

THE EARTH ANGEL'S HEALING GUIDE:

TRUST YOUR SENSES

WORLDLY PROBLEMS. COSMIC SOLUTIONS!

TRUST YOUR SENSES

I came across a grand opportunity to attend a Legacy retreat in the Bahamas. For months I said to myself, "I'm going to the Bahamas, to SHIFT into my legacy!".

A week before the trip, I had to meet with the organizer for an interview. I showed up as my Full Potential & of course I passed & got accepted into the program, Yayyyyy!

I already packed my bags and bought a plane ticket for $59 <u>BEFORE</u> being accepted.

There were a few glitches… I hadn't received funds yet to pay for as an attendee of the week long program. In addition, my plane ticket was only a one-way ticket, therefore I had NO CLUE on how the fuck I was getting back home.

> *Yet STILL I told myself every day,*
> *"I'm going to the Bahamas, to SHIFT into my legacy!"*

Days before my flight to The Bahamas, I started feeling exceptionally anxious, overwhelmed and began contemplating canceling this trip & staying home… In my comfort zone.

I became distracted with reasons why I shouldn't go…
"My hair wasn't done."
"My toes weren't done and they were falling off."
"I need to buy new outfits."
"How am I flying home?"
"Need money to pay for the retreat?"

My thoughts and feelings of self-doubt or self-judgment couldn't even be endorsed with such resistance because it was my Spirit that interrupted these low vibrations so boldly, so courageously to me stating
" **GET YOUR ASS ON THE PLANE!** ".

I was not required to buy anything or do anything else other than MOVE WITH PURPOSE!

I detached from toxicity and without fear or discouragement, I got all this ass on that plane & flew to Nassau, Bahamas.

As my true self.
Of my Full Potential.
Without resistance.

I trusted with all my heart and soul that the God I hold such a unique relationship with will provide all that's REQUIRED for me to BE PRESENT at this retreat.

TRUST YOUR SENSES

It was the vibration of gratitude as well as the universal Law of Action activated within me as the will of God, through the spirit of faith that got me to The Bahamas. Creating a Divine rhythm of flow, dignity and gratefulness in my life that officially launched my nonprofit organization All Is Mind International. AIM expands the youthfulness of the mind, body & spirit with a mission to live with purpose as love and divine joy.

Over the seven days in this legacy retreat I realized all that I inquired, when it comes to building a brand logistically for my organization was already done. It essentially called for some fine tuning. By allowing my physical body to get still in such a beautiful space, resting my mind from all other worldly problems and focusing solely on PURPOSE, I was able to radiate a new beginning audaciously launching AIM.

Oh! I was able to spend an extra day in The Bahamas, bought my ticket the day before to fly home, ANDDD the same day I got back home… (deposit available) paid for the legacy retreat program in full!!

SHIFT Happens as you decide to own your SHIFT.
Lean into the unexpected.
Trust your inner guidance.
Trusting the voice that propels you outside of your comfort zone.

Gratitude is the Altitude!

Applying the universal law of action revealed in me
the Spirit of God as the co-creating I AM PRESENCE.

This feeling of goodwill.
This energy of harmony.
This is a manifestation of good fortune.
Streamlined ALL that was required to sustain,
the highest vibration within & the good of ALL!

As I Affirm, Declare and Decree:
I AM ALL THAT GOD IS, GOD IS ALL THAT I AM

TRUST YOUR SENSES

EXERCISE: What had happened was…

GOAL:

☐ When was the last time you took a leap of FAITH?

ASK YOURSELF - Think of the craziest thing you've ever done in your life. When? With who? How did you feel, Before & After? Has the experience allowed you to be MORE confident with the decisions you make in your life?

_____

_____

_____

_____

_____

_____

_____

_____

_____

_____

_____

_____

_____

_____

_____

_____

_____

_____

TRUST YOUR SENSES

THE EARTH ANGEL'S HEALING GUIDE:

NOTES

WORLDLY PROBLEMS. COSMIC SOLUTIONS!

COME HOLY SPIRIT COME!

Download Your FREE Bookmark:
[Master Your Mind, Master Your Life](https://acrobat.adobe.com/link/track?uri=urn:aaid:scds:US:10adab99-f7d6-34dd-968c-453937b4cd07)
https://acrobat.adobe.com/link/track?uri=urn:aaid:scds:US:10adab99-f7d6-34dd-968c-453937b4cd07

Download Your FREE Mind Map:
[See Your Voice | Mind Map](https://acrobat.adobe.com/link/track?uri=urn:aaid:scds:US:e827a5b9-1d58-36f2-a89e-66c91dceb021)
https://acrobat.adobe.com/link/track?uri=urn:aaid:scds:US:e827a5b9-1d58-36f2-a89e-66c91dceb021

Listen To Your FREE Archangel Meditations:
[The Archangel Channel](https://youtube.com/playlist?list=PL4E_BwuM5MaL_xCu9R_WibrbyNNGjPIhA)
https://youtube.com/playlist?list=PL4E_BwuM5MaL_xCu9R_WibrbyNNGjPIhA

NOTES

NOTES

NOTES

NOTES

NOTES

NOTES

NOTES

GLOSSARY

- **Baneful Attachments** - Toxic energetic & harmful spiritual bonds

- **BE-ing** - Your actions & energy

- **Body** - Our beliefs, thoughts & actions carried out by our **Vessel**

- **Defense Mechanisms** - Physical blocks & self-sabotaging barriers that prevent spiritual growth

- **Escapism** - unnecessary people, illusions, fantasies & distractions that prevent or determine from their purpose and/or focus

- **Full Potential** - Showing up in the world with purpose with all that you say, in all that you do, as all that you are

- **INNER-standing** - A divine connection with the soul's purpose & mission

- **Mind** - How we conceptualize thought & hidden triggers into the **Spirit** of Gratitude

- **Mind-Full-N.E.S.S** - A state of oneness by which you connect with God's inner guidance

- **Our Spirit** - Divine experiences of BE-ing; Personified as the **Essence** of our attitude

- **Soul** - Embodiment of our BE-ing; Perceptualize as the frequency shift unto our **Mindset**

- **Soul Talk** - Mental & emotional talks of self-discipline with wholeness & oneness

- **Source Energy** - A Divine connection with God in your physical body

The Earth Angel's Healing Guide:

IT IS QUITE THE LANDING
WHEN WE ZOOM DOWN TO EARTH
AND THEN ALL OF A SUDDEN,
WE FORGET THAT WE HAVE
THESE WINGS!!!

THROUGH A STATE OF REMEMBRANCE,
VIA PRAYER
(IN WHICH WE TALK TO GOD)
& MEDITATION
(WHICH REQUIRES ONE TO LISTEN),

WE CAN CHOOSE
TO UNLEARN AS WE ARE TAUGHT,
THEN RELEARN AS WE EXPERIENCE...
THE PURE VIBRATION
OF LOVE AND RELATIONSHIP
WITH SPIRIT AS SPIRIT.

THE SUBCONSCIOUS MIND TRANSCENDS INTO POSITIVE THOUGHT FORMS THROUGH MANY ALTERNATIVE PATHWAYS, YET ACCORDING TO YOUR SOUL MISSION THERE IS ONLY ONE RITUAL THAT CAPTIVATES AND SUSTAINS HIGH VIBRATIONAL ENERGY VIA OUR THOUGHTS THAT MAY BE MANIFESTED INTO THE PRESENT REALITY.

SELF-LOVE IS A FUNDAMENTAL PILLAR TO UNIVERSAL HARMONIZATION. THIS TRUE NATURE OF BE-ING & HEALING, MAY BE UTILIZED TO GUIDE OUR THOUGHTS & INSPIRED ACTIONS INTO HEALING RITUALS AND SPIRITUAL NOT JUST PERSONAL DEVELOPMENT.

PRETTY MUCH, INSTEAD OF FOCUSING ON "WHY ME?" OR "BEING NEGATIVE NANCY OR NICK", WE CAN CHOOSE TO INVITE OUR DESIRED NARRATIVE WITHIN THE MINDSET, SEE BEYOND THE CIRCUMSTANCES & APPLY INSPIRED ACTION.

IN ESSENCE, WITH DAILY EVOLUTION WE MANAGE TO
"KEEP OUR VIBRATIONS HIGH & UNNECESSARY ATTACHMENTS LOW!"

Worldy Problems.
Cosmic Solutions!

FAITHFUL SENSE LLC©
PUBLICATIONS

www.ingramcontent.com/pod-product-compliance
Lightning Source LLC
Chambersburg PA
CBHW050241120526
44590CB00016B/2180